Judith Halbreich's lifetime of advocacy work is focused on the importance of all children having a home base and continuous mentorship. She is a licensed clinical social worker and psychotherapist with a successful executive career in social services, clinical research, and mental health. Judith is the founder of Home of Champions, a unique program in Upstate New York that identifies leaders emerging from the foster care system and supports them towards becoming champions of their best selves. Judith is Mary's oldest daughter.

To the memory of my mother, Mary, and to my dear fellow adopted sister, Janet.

Judith Halbreich

THE AUDACITY TO BE DIVINE

A Soul's Journey Towards Illumination

AUSTIN MACAULEY PUBLISHERS™

LONDON • CAMBRIDGE • NEW YORK • SHARJAH

Ordering Information:
Quantity sales: special discounts are available on quantity purchases by corporations, associations, and others. For details, contact the publisher at the address below.

Publisher's Cataloging-in-Publication data
Halbreich, Judith
The Audacity to be Divine

ISBN 9781645363613 (Paperback)
ISBN 9781645363620 (Hardback)
ISBN 9781645368984 (ePub e-book)

Library of Congress Control Number: 2020906423

www.austinmacauley.com/us

First Published (2020)
Austin Macauley Publishers LLC
40 Wall Street, 28th Floor
New York, NY 10005
USA

mail-usa@austinmacauley.com
+1 (646) 5125767

Citations are taken from Mary's letters to the author, including journals, videos, and audio videos. All quotations from the Bible are taken from the Revised Standard Version Catholic Edition.

I would like to thank the many people who allowed themselves to be interviewed for this book, including Francis Bove, Peter Caparaso, Mary Dwyer, David Frenette, father, Thomas Keating, Joan Kovacs, Anne Mazza, and sister, Bernadette Teasdale. I want to extend my thanks to Wendy Lee and a great appreciation to Martin Rowe of Lantern Books for working so hard and with such skill on this manuscript.

I also wish to thank my husband and our lovely daughter, Bethany, for their support for this project, which has now been two decades in the making, and for retaining their faith in me and the book when both of us were a little shaky!

Writing a book about close family members is always a trial for the family and friends, and I'm aware that some of you reading this book will find it hard to recognize the Mary you grew up with or the Mary who's portrayed between these covers. Please know that all of you who were deeply involved with her life—particularly the lifelong friends that she made and who were so supportive of her and my sister and me growing up—were deeply loved by Mary, and that Janet and I are more appreciative than we can say for the help you provided us with, as a family and individually. My mother considered Janet and me the greatest gifts that she had received in her life, and I feel precisely that way about my sister. Janet: I realize that this book has been very hard for you. Please know that I wrote it out of love and compassion, to get to the heart of what motivated our mother, and to explain, if only to myself, the fierce devotion that drove her relentlessly toward God.

Table of Contents

"I am where I need to be. Everything around me includes and hides the sacred."
—*Mary Mrozowski (1926-1993)*

"I never thought I'd hear God speak with a Brooklyn accent."
—*Al Choy (1993)*

Foreword

Thomas Keating

"To the family of Mary and all of Mary's friends: My heart is completely broken because I've lost, as it were, both arms, but above all, my heart is completely gone because Mary died. Mary and I had a most extraordinary friendship. It's a friendship that tells me something about the Communion of Saints that nothing else has done in my life. I'm not really sad, I'm just shocked, like I've been hit by a truck, so to speak. I'm sure that you understand that feeling.

I can't believe that Mary is gone. There's something in me that refuses to accept that fact on a natural level, and yet in the meantime, we must celebrate. With God's help, I'll try to give you just a bit of history on how Mary's life has unfolded, especially in my presence. Of course, I've seen it from a perspective that maybe many of you have not, although your view is just as valuable.

She showed up at a retreat I gave in New Mexico, sent by Sr. Thelma Hall, her spiritual director who was also a friend of mine and who wanted us to get together. Well, we got together all right, and we never recovered. I could see in Mary right away the embodiment of the vision I have for Contemplative Outreach, the vision of sharing with laypersons and folks in active ministry the profound inner meaning of monastic life that should never have been locked into a cloister someplace, that belongs to lay men and women by the fact of their baptism, their confirmation. It's Christ in you, leading your life, and in complete solidarity with your life, just as it includes the dark side of your sins. The meaning of Jesus incarnate is that he has come to share your life and to live it for you, with you, and in you.

Now, Mary already had that intuition. She had been working with the divorced Catholics. In those days, divorced Catholics were not at the top of the list in the Church. So she gave them some honor—she was a divorced lady herself—and then she moved on to Bible-study and then she was with the Charismatic Renewal. Then she drove out to join us in this retreat, which was a kind of watershed, and from that time on, I kept asking Mary to join us in some further work.

First it was with teaching centering prayer. Centering prayer is only a way of entering contemplative prayer, which itself is just a way of relating to God permanently instead of just saying hello on Sunday or grace at meals. This life of God in us starts growing, growing, growing so that it lives in us and it becomes a permanent thing. This was the way that Mary was growing, step by step. Spiritual life is a growth process, growing up in God so wherever you are now is just a new beginning. It has unlimited possibilities.

I said to Mary, "Would you help me with centering prayer?"

She said, "I can't afford it because I have to earn a living, and I don't have any time."

There was another gentleman on the retreat who said, "I'll pay Mary a full salary and she can work three full days for you."

That's how in this Long Island, New York area, she began to have time to work with us. Then when we saw, we needed a structure to support the people who were doing centering prayer, support groups, and so forth, and I asked her if she would be the executive director of a little organization that we started calling Contemplative Outreach, and she said okay. I didn't ask any questions what else she was doing; I just wanted that okay.

Then another year later, we had the opportunity to start a living community which would incarnate the vision of Contemplative Outreach, to provide a place where people could come and receive the unadulterated figure of an interior life, of the life of prayer, so that they could bring it back into their daily life and begin to incorporate it into the day.

This involved living in a rather down-at-the-heel house with two young men who were only one step away from being hippies. They have somewhat improved over the years. One of them is still with us. And she said, "Let's do it, let's do it." She wasn't the kind of girl to hang back at this point, and they finally settled down in what you now know as Warwick, New York.

But the thing that is so important about Mary, it seems to me, is that she embodies a lay contemplative saint. I mean saint, because all this business of plaster-statues and whatnot and icons, but as far as I'm concerned, this is for the birds. I want to see somebody with flesh and blood who is in love with God, and who says so, and who empowers other people to experience their potentiality for this same romance, this relationship. Prayer is not prayers, prayer is not formulas; prayer is relationship, a relationship that keeps growing, expanding, deepening, and becoming dynamic. There's no telling where it's going to go, there's no telling what the Lord will call you to if you're open.

We base our centering prayer on three theological principles. It's Trinitarian at its source. It's rooted in the faith that this God of the universe is the ultimate reality. It's living God's own life within us. This sharing and intimate love between relationships is the divine Trinity, and then we're pulled into that dynamic of giving and receiving. It becomes more and more unlimited because God is unlimited, and it's crystal logical in its focus. That means that as we do contemplative prayer or centering prayer, which is a way into it, we participate on the deepest level in the past. Here, the unloading of the unconscious and the trials of prayer become our share of Christ's passion within and prepares us to bear the trial of daily life which is no longer difficult but part of the journey, and part of our sharing and retention of the world. It doesn't look like much from the outside, but inside, this welcoming, this acceptance of our innermost trials and joys of daily life, is the divine life manifesting itself in our littleness, in our weakness, and I dare say, even at times in our sinfulness.

Finally, that third source of contemplative prayer is bonding. It's ecclesiastical in its effects. Ecclesiastical doesn't mean just coming to church; it means feeling your union and unity with everyone in the world, especially the poor and those in need and those you love. It's these three things that make contemplative prayer transforming.

I'm not asking you to remember these three things, I'm only saying that Mary, in my view, was embodied in each of those three things. The Trinity, her love of Christ, and the bonding. Now, the bonding has two parts, two subdivisions: one is personal enhancement of your whole life. Whatever you have gets bigger, even if it's your debts. Everything gets bigger, your love of your family, your capacity to relate to others. Mary was leading a kind of quasi-contemplative life. We deliberately never make it a religious life, because we wanted it for laypersons, and it was the layperson that we are trying to call or empower to take possession of their baptismal grace, to become what religious should be, namely the manifestation of the God of love in daily life.

Now, I noticed that Mary, as a result of five or six hours of centering prayer a day for seven or eight years, in addition to what she did before, was increasing her love of her family. She was becoming the happiest Grandma on earth. She was loving her daughters more and more, and she was relating to her brothers and sisters. This was becoming a community problem, because how do you fulfill your duties in the community and outside at the same time? That's your problem too. But with Contemplative Outreach, this group is trying to come to grips with how you do that. You don't leave prayer and you don't leave your duties. You don't leave your husband or your wife because you're becoming holy. You come to peace with everything, and this personal enhancement has, what I would conclude, what seems to me, the most marvelous quality of Mary's.

What I would like to leave you with is this extraordinary quality of empowerment. By that, I mean the bonding, the bonding with God that becomes so exuberant that everything she was doing was becoming a prayer. Sr. Bernadette was there on her deathbed. They had been praying all day long, and Mary was saying, "If we go in the next room, that's prayer. If we sit down, that's prayer. If we have eggs and bacon, that's our prayer. If we go to dessert, that's our prayer." Prayer is not so much what you do, it's why you do it and who you do it. In other words, it's all coming out the center that has gradually become established. A center that is always ready, ready for God's will, always willing. From that perspective, dying is no problem, except for your relatives and friends.

Some of you have heard some of my tapes and you remember the story of Bernie O'Shea who was giving, giving, giving, and who was always ready to do God's will. In a single moment, he fell dead on the street in Aspen because there was no need to delay, there was no need for preparation, no need for holy water. There's a point in which they've done their work and you have the sacrament of the church, whatever you do is pouring grace into the world. This is the fruit, not just of a religious life, but a life out of a baptism and confirmation, fully understood through the eye of faith, enlightened by contemplative prayer.

It's this eye of faith enlightened by contemplative prayer that Mary was giving to everybody in the last years of her life and getting better at it all the time. I saw that she had reached the peak of her ministry and I was willing to let her go out of Chrysalis House and spend her whole time on her duties, but she didn't want to do that. The discernment she made with the support of her wonderful community was to provide her with a chance to do that as much as she wanted to, and that's what she was doing when she died. As we say in the west, she died with her boots on, or should I say, with her booties on. She just never stopped loving God.

Death is not an interruption. Throughout our network and beyond, I'm getting wonderful feedback that even though it's a terrible shock, somehow you feel the presence of God. We feel the joy of Mary; we feel her empowerment through all this. In other words, the Communion of Saints knows no boundaries. If we are on the same wavelength in any degree that Mary was on, our grief, our joy, our grief today is going to be taken into an even greater joy at the sense of what she did.

A laywoman, divorced, a woman with a very difficult life, a woman in various ministries but always growing, a woman who is now a classical example of a lay-contemplative person. Maybe there are others, but I don't know anybody of this quality yet. This, to me, is the very heart and soul of the second valuable counsel, the spiritual renewal, especially the empowerment of laypeople to take charge of the church, to take charge of this mission, and to take charge of this spiritual direction which, I'm sorry to say, few of the clergy are trained to do. That's why they're diminishing, but the spirit is raising up laypersons who are more and more capable of providing the church with the interior spirit that it has to survive into the next century.

I'm going to miss Mary terribly, as you will. I can't see how to go on without her, but I know by faith that she hasn't finished her job. St. Therese of Lisieux said, "I'm going to spend my heaven doing good upon earth. I'm not just going to sit around up there doing nothing, when everybody else is in trouble."

The fact is that Mary was interrupted so suddenly in the midst of a tremendous ministry. She was a smashing success in Denver and people were hanging all over her to get her advice, and she just slipped away from us with no delays, like Bernie O'Shea. I think she one-upped Bernie O'Shea, because not only did she accept death, but as you know, her great philosophy was to welcome death or the ending event, and someone who welcomes death welcomes God.

So whatever she is up to at the moment, I don't think she is sitting around. She's active, she's speaking to us on the new level, and to be tuned into that new level, you have only to pray, to do your own form of contemplative prayer, and I predict that Mary's death is not the end of something, but she's the lay example of St. Therese of Lisieux. She's not doing it from a cloister, she'll be with you in the street, at the kitchen sink, and if necessary, in bed.

Once again, my deepest sympathy to the family and to the members of Chrysalis House. May God be with us all and may we in our sorrow, be turned into joy, and to go now and do likewise."

—Fr. Thomas Keating
St. Dominic's Church, Oyster Bay, Long Island,
October 23, 1993.

Introduction

"I never thought I'd hear God speak with a Brooklyn accent," said an admiring follower. That sums up the life journey of Mary Mrozowski—an ordinary woman who transformed herself to an extraordinary spiritual leader.

The last time I saw my mother, Mary Mrozowski, was on a crisp, cool afternoon in early October, 1993. I was traveling with my three-year-old daughter, Bethany, back from New York City to our home in Buffalo. My mother suggested that we visit her at Chrysalis House, a communal faith retreat in Warwick, about sixty miles outside of the city.

"That's out of my way, Mom," I said to her. "I want to get back home by nightfall."

"Please, Judy," my mother pleaded. "It's really important that I see you."

I can't say how glad I am that I acceded to my mother's request. As always, she knew best. Maybe at that time, she sensed that this would be the final opportunity for us to talk to each other.

At sixty-seven years old, Mother had spent the past eight years of her life in the lay contemplative community at Chrysalis House, fine-tuning practices such as the Welcoming Prayer that would become hallmarks of what we now know as the centering prayer movement—the three-decades-long attempt to revive the mystical contemplative tradition within Christianity and offer an alternative to those who were seeking meditative practices in the Asian religious traditions. Although Mary spent most of her time in community, leading retreats and workshops, and providing individuals with spiritual guidance, she was in constant demand as a speaker. At this point in her life, my mother had never been happier, more energetic, or certain of her faith. Indeed, when she greeted us at the front door at Chrysalis House, she appeared radiant, filled with an inner light that was almost otherworldly.

It was easy to ignore that her arm was still in a sling. Over the summer, I had invited Mother on a trip to Italy with my family. The trip had proceeded smoothly until one day, on a narrow cobblestone street in Palermo, Sicily, a speeding car had knocked my mother to the ground and fractured her arm. Despite being in terrible pain, Mary drew on her inner strength to welcome the physical sensation and overcome the will to fight it. The doctors and nurses were amazed that she refused any painkillers, but that was the mother I knew. The Spirit was so strong in her that she could even conquer pain.

Now, at Chrysalis House, I asked Mother about her arm. In a few days, she was scheduled to go to Colorado, where she was to lead a spiritual retreat.

"Don't you think the high altitude will make it harder for you to cope with your arm?" I inquired, worried.

"Oh, Judith, just let it go," my mother said. "Where is your faith? You grew up knowing all of the Beatles lyrics, but do you know any of the scriptures?"

Whenever my mother started asking me whether I knew my scriptures, I could tell she was doing fine. Still, I couldn't help worrying about her traveling so soon after her accident.

In the afternoon, we ate lunch and chatted. Then she took Bethany by the hand and they walked down to the lake in the back of the house to feed the ducks. As we were leaving, I rolled down the car-door window, "Mom, I'll call you soon."

She nodded and waved.

I was never able to make that call.

Mother died a week later on Monday, October 18, 1993. The Friday night before, she was giving a talk in Georgetown, Colorado. This last retreat started as the others had over the previous years. Two coordinators of this particular event, who were not familiar with Mary's charisma or passion, were assuming that the retreat would be, if not exactly humdrum, then uneventful. *"But when Mary first opened her mouth,"* wrote one of them, *"she seemed to know that this workshop would be different. She was so clear and so alive Friday night, and so radiating God's love that we were all encompassed by it."* My mother talked about her broken arm and how she had surrendered to God in the moment, letting go of her physical suffering without painkillers, aspirin, or expectations. God, she reported, had given her the clarity to be present to what needed to be done and had sent the angels to assist. The crowd was as astonished to hear this as the medical

21

professionals had been, when they set her arm with nothing but her faith to alleviate the agony.

As she stood at the podium that October, Mary made a striking figure. She was wearing her favorite red suit (my gift to her), high heels, and dangling earrings. Her perfectly manicured nails were painted to match her outfit. As someone once observed, Mary always looked like a million bucks, even though she lived on a meager budget. She enjoyed dressing up for her audience, whether they were retreat attendees or inmates in the prison ministry she was involved with. Indeed, she considered it a means of showing those to whom she was speaking that she cared enough about herself and them to make an effort to be more than presentable. *"She was a stunning woman,"* wrote the coordinator of that final retreat, *"sensuous, charismatic, and articulate, and [she] had a way about her that made every word coming out of her mouth sound like it was a word coming from the mouth of God."*

By this stage in Mary's ministry, many people wanted to speak to her. During the break, according to witnesses, she stepped back to avoid the surging and enthusiastic crowd and fell, hitting her head on the edge of the podium. After a few minutes of unconsciousness, she woke up and informed the concerned onlookers that she was fine. "God is so good," she whispered. She asked the audience to leave her for a minute while she collected herself and returned to her practice. Remarkably to my mind, no one demanded that she go to the hospital. No one even insisted that she stop the retreat.

Over the next two days, Mary led prayer practice, answered questions, and gave individual people spiritual guidance that affirmed and captivated them. Mary dazzled attendees with her insights—a situation that was now customary. "Mary can see right into my heart," observed one former retreatant in awe. Another wrote that her marriage had been falling apart and that the practices Mary presented led to a turning point in her life. Yet another admitted that she'd confessed to my mother that her heart wasn't in her work anymore (she had taught school for thirty years). Mother had replied: "Put your heart in your work, then you'll have the freedom to make choices." This advice had surprised the teacher, but had inspired her to continue to find joy in her profession. As one participant summarized: "Mary's words were wisdom words."

The Monday following the Colorado retreat, Mary was visiting the home of her friend, Sr. Bernadette Teasdale. The two women had been praying all morning and had just taken lunch. Then, without warning, a jolt appeared to sweep through my mother's body and she slid from the armchair to the floor. Sr. Bernadette reported that Mary recovered briefly, asked, "What happened?" and then closed her eyes. This time, she didn't regain consciousness.

Mother's funeral mass took place at St. Dominic's Church in Oyster Bay, New York. Three priests served and her long-time friend, Fr. Thomas Keating, depleted and shaken, addressed the congregation.

"My heart is completely broken," he mourned, his voice wavering. "I can't believe that she is gone. There is something in me that refuses to accept that fact." As he continued to tell the story of how Mary had come into his life, and how the very unlikely bond between a divorcée from Queens and a Trappist monk had been forged, the church was hushed, a silence broken only by the occasional sigh and quiet sob coming from family and friends.

Fr. Keating told the congregation that my mother embodied "a lay contemplative saint… Somebody with flesh and blood who is in love with God and who says so, and who empowers other people to experience their potentiality for the same romance, this relationship with God." In her love of Christ and her capacity to relate to others, Mary was, he observed, expressing the full nature of the lay-contemplative life—someone at the very peak of her powers, and yet, also a woman continuing to grow and expand in her love for her family, her friends, and the entire religious community that had sprung up around her and that she was both absorbed by and encompassed.

"I am going to miss Mary terribly," Fr. Keating concluded, "as you will. I can't see how to go on without her, but I know by faith that she hasn't finished her job." He noted that the French Discalced Carmelite nun, St. Therese of Lisieux, known as 'The Little Flower of Jesus,' had reported that she would spend her time in heaven doing good upon Earth, and that she wouldn't be sitting around simply doing nothing when everybody else was in trouble. Mary had been, what he called, "a smashing success in Denver," and that her 'slipping away,' as he termed it, was not so much an ending event as a welcoming of God.

* * *

My mother died doing what she loved best—looking directly into people's hearts and assuring them that God was listening to them. The surrender, attentiveness, and humility required to practice this level of discernment were qualities that had required a lifetime's development—a lifetime filled with heartbreak and triumph, daily suffering and enlightenment, soul-searching and a period of deep despair when she almost lost her faith entirely. What she underwent in her sixty-seven years would have been unbearable for some people, but for my mother, it only strengthened her resolve and belief in the goodness of God.

My mother's spiritual journey began at the age of four, when her grandmother started taking her to church in Jamaica, Queens. Her childhood with an inept mother and an alcoholic, abusive father made home-life difficult, but she found refuge in the church, uplifted by the sacred rites of Communion and Confirmation. She was highly intelligent, but her father forced her to dropout before her last year of high-school to start working and bring money into the family.

At twenty-one, she married a neighborhood boy, Joseph Mrozowski. She looked forward to becoming a mother, but a botched surgery resulted in her being unable to bear biological children. Fate stepped in and she adopted two daughters, myself and my younger sister, Janet. She always believed there was no child in need who couldn't be helped in some way. Yet in doing so, she came closer than perhaps even she imagined, to bringing disaster upon our family.

After twenty years of marriage, her life collapsed: my father asked for a divorce. Angry, ashamed, and humiliated, my mother retreated to the basement of our house in Plainview, Long Island, where she took in ironing to earn a living for the next several years. Here, in what she referred to in her lectures as her 'cave' or 'tomb,' she began the long and ultimately miraculous transformation that would eventually allow her to let go of her rage and restore her faith in God.

In 1970, my mother helped establish the Long Island Chapter of Separated and Divorced Catholics. "When I divorced, I didn't have a problem—the Church did!" she was known to say. She believed that, perhaps more than anyone else, these people needed love and reassurance that God had not forgotten them. Out of this chapter, she established a Bible Study group that continued for thirteen years. During this time, she led workshops that helped people to let go of their attachments and form prayer groups. On the outside, she was a single mother of two teenage girls, working as a medical administrator. On the inside, her faith and her understanding of her own abilities were growing by leaps and bounds.

Crucial to this spiritual development was my mother's joining of the Charismatic Renewal on Long Island, which had begun in the late 1960s. Through her engagement with this movement, she was introduced to centering prayer, which had been started in the 1970s by Fr. Thomas Keating, Fr. William Meninger, and Fr. Basil Pennington, who'd begun the practice when all three were resident at St. Joseph's Abbey in Spencer, Massachusetts. Following the advice of her spiritual director, Mary took part in an intensive two-week retreat in New Mexico held by Fr. Keating in 1983. Fr. Keating was so impressed with her that he asked her to help him establish Contemplative Outreach, an organization devoted to the practice of centering prayer. My mother developed her well-regarded and transformative Open Mind Open Heart workshops, and ended up serving as the first executive director of the organization, remaining on its board of directors until her death.

In 1985, Fr. Keating asked my mother to do something astonishing—to abandon her current life and establish an experimental live-in community with two young men. My mother eventually agreed and gave away all her possessions. This is how Chrysalis House was born. Living in Chrysalis House was a huge challenge for my mother. She was used to being in charge, whereas here, she had to deal with difficult personalities in a monastic setting. She gained some relief when she traveled. She also became part of a prison ministry, visiting inmates at Eastern Correctional Facility in Warwick, New York. Through her interaction with the prisoners, she found herself experiencing, at long last, unconditional love. From her prison ministry, she was also able to find the strength to forgive her father and (in the last year of her life) finally free herself from the threat of violence that shadowed her.

Mother was a mother to many people in her life. From childhood, she brought up her four younger siblings. When she wasn't able to become a biological mother, she adopted two daughters and fostered many more children. With the Long Island Chapter of Separated and Divorced Catholics, her Bible Study, and other groups, she helped people along their own spiritual journey. With Fr. Keating, she laid the foundations for Contemplative Outreach and helped create the organization it is today. Through the prison ministry, she spread the message of God's ever-present love for us all. Her friend, Mary Dwyer, who lived with her at Chrysalis House, recounted, "Mary was like the ace you carry in your back-pocket. I'd always think to myself, if I ever really got in trouble, I could always ask Mary and she'd tell me what to do. It's like that Beatles song [Let It Be], 'Speaking words of wisdom.' There was always Mother Mary to go to."

* * *

It has been more than twenty years since my mother left us, but there isn't a day that goes by that I don't think about her or speak her name. I've no doubt that, like Therese of Lisieux, Mary is busy working to alleviate misery and heartbreak from heaven, continuing to inspire me, my family, and the people whose lives she touched in ways that cannot be measured and perhaps, in a manner that even we who knew her don't recognize.

That said, those of us still on Earth sometimes need to be nudged toward God a little more directly, which is why I decided to create this book! My mother had always wanted to write a memoir, but her life was cut short. Luckily, she left behind journals, lectures, and testimonials that have provided some insight into the journey that she undertook, both physically through this world and spiritually. For that reason, in this book, I've opted to use the first person, as if she were still here in the room with us. I've relied heavily on my own memories, as well as interviews with relatives and my mother's friends and colleagues, to fill in any remaining gaps. I've also changed some names to protect identities and abbreviated some episodes to allow the story to proceed more smoothly. The effect, I'm hoping, is to create less of a biography and more of a portrait come to life—with all the ordinariness and extraordinariness that attends everyone's life.

In shaping *Mary of Chrysalis House*, I've sometimes had to rely on my own intuitions not only as to what my mother was thinking at that time, but perhaps even those feelings and thoughts that remained hidden to herself. For much of her life, Mary was tightly wound and controlling. She could be brusque and direct to the point of rudeness. The psychological patterns that were laid out in her early life by her parents continued to reassert themselves in her marriage and with her children, and even in Chrysalis House. Sometimes these patterns were not visible to her, as they were to her daughters.

There were many reasons why these behaviors recurred: an alcoholic father, a feckless mother, a childhood marked by responsibilities no child should have to bear, a troubled marriage, and then the struggle for money and self-determination. But one reason, argues Thomas Keating, for behavior such as Mary's is fundamental to the human condition and the development of what he terms 'the false self': the child's wish to assert power and control, seek survival and security, and express her need for affection and esteem. These 'programs for happiness,' as he terms them, may be fundamental to the survival of the infant, but to our detriment, we hold on to them into our mature years. They then affect our attitudes we have to ourselves and those around us, and most importantly, our relationship with God.

It is the task of the spiritual journey, Keating observes, to grapple with the false self by allowing God—the Divine Therapist—to enter into the soul through the means of centering prayer, and disturb and reprogram those programs for happiness. Such a process is, in many ways, lifelong; its progress is not necessarily linear or made easier by a formal commitment to the spiritual life. This book, therefore, also serves, through Mary's life, as an exploration of the possibilities of divine therapy as a means of locating and releasing our false selves: of growing up and into a mature and humble relationship with a loving and infinitely forgiving God.

For those of you who had the good fortune to know Mary, the revelations about her childhood and adult struggles might deepen your understanding of her. For those of you who didn't, I want to present her in her many dimensions, as a living, breathing human being who wrestled with the difficulties of her life and in her final few years, released them in a way that can be a lesson to us all.

The thousands who attended and celebrated at her funeral loved her. They adored her as earth mother. They loved her as spiritual mother, as someone they can aspire to be.

Part I Setting the Focus

1 Joy

"Wake up, Marie," my grandmother says. "It's time to go to church."

I am four years old. Half asleep, I stumble out of bed and get dressed. Outside, in the early morning, my grandmother takes my hand in her own—warm and comforting and kind. We walk down the street as our neighborhood in Jamaica, Queens, starts to come to life. On Sutphin Boulevard, Mrs. Kapp is setting clothes and blankets in the windows of her store. Mr. Cohen is sweeping the sidewalk in front of his grocer's shop. People are lined up at the curb to take the bus to their jobs in Manhattan, about an hour and a half away.

In the 1920s and '30s, Jamaica, Queens, was a primarily Italian, Polish, and African American working-class neighborhood. Over the years, the population had grown not only because of new immigrants, but because the elevated rail line had been extended from Manhattan into Queens in 1918. The busiest street in the area was Jamaica Avenue, where you could find department stores such as Gertz and Macy's.

"*Andiamo*, Marie, *andiamo*," my grandmother says to me in Italian. "Let's go."

After my grandmother and I cross Sutphin Boulevard, the neighborhood grows quiet again. Rows of detached and semi-detached houses just like our own line both sides of the street. We turn the corner onto Liverpool Street and head toward St. Pius V Church. Huge to a child, its tall, white face with two statues and carvings looms underneath a peaked roof. St. Pius V, for whom the church was named, became Pope in the mid-sixteenth century and was a leader of the Catholic Counter-Reformation.

My family's parish church was actually St. Monica's near Jamaica Avenue, but we always worshipped at St. Pius because it was closer. Down Sutphin Boulevard was another Roman Catholic Church, St. Joseph's. This church served the Polish community and was even bigger than St. Pius. Of the three local churches, St. Monica's was the oldest. St. Monica's was established in 1856, while St. Pius and St. Joseph's had both been built in the early 1900s.

Still holding my hand, my grandmother leads me through St. Pius' double-doors. We enter into a sacred space filled with music and the smell of burning candles.

* * *

This routine with my grandmother occurred on many occasions when I was a young child. Of course, I didn't know what was being intoned or sung. I didn't understand why a carved wooden man was on a cross at the front of the room, his arms outstretched. Who was he reaching out to? Was it to me? When I lifted my head, I could see the arched ceiling made up of little paintings. If I turned my head left or right, I could see the colorful, stained, glass windows.

The same man appeared in these windows, standing among people who were kneeling at his feet.

I felt warm and secure, like I was being held by God. A feeling flooded through me, similar to the warmth from my grandmother's hand and the sunlight shining through the windows. It was something like joy.

After Mass, my grandmother would take me around the neighborhood to visit the poor—often newly arrived immigrants from Italy and Poland. We'd bring them baskets containing clothes, food, and diapers for the babies. There were so many babies. I'd hold them in my arms and think about the babies I might have someday.

Once, on the way back home, I asked, "Doña, why do we visit these people?" 'Doña' was what everyone called my grandmother, because she had such a powerful presence in the community.

"Because, Mary," my grandmother replied, "we must help others as God would."

At the time, I didn't appreciate what she meant. What did these raggedly dressed, hungry people have to do with God? I know now that my grandmother practiced what she preached. She set the example I would try to follow for the rest of my life. My grandmother was the one who put me on the path of my spiritual journey, through her conditioning, her service, and her love for God. Her example, for better or worse, remained with me forever.

Although my grandmother still spoke Italian, she'd lived in America for years. Her daughter, my mother, Gianna Casabona, had been born here. My father, Giovanni Caporaso, was born in 1899 in the small town of Pietrelcina, located in the province of Benevento in the south of Italy, about thirty miles north of Naples. In 1923, he arrived in New York City.

As the story goes, my father met my mother when she was only fourteen years old. With her long, curly red hair, my mother was a very beautiful girl. You can see it in her Confirmation photograph, taken when she was around ten years old. However, she still looks like a child, so it's hard to believe that just a few years later, she would become a wife. My parents ran away together during her school break. When the truant officer arrived at her house to ask why she hadn't gone to school, my grandmother could only say helplessly, "She got married." Given how young my mother was, and how unprepared she was for marriage, I find it strange that my grandmother did not put up more resistance to the arrangement. Certainly, nobody talked about whether it was appropriate, let alone legal (it was), for a man who was thirteen years older than a minor to marry. But the Italian community in Queens was very tight-knit and insular, and I imagine it served both families, who knew each other, to ensure that whatever had occurred before the wedding would be made respectable through a marriage.

The truth is that, for my mother, marriage was an escape from a volatile and verbally and physically abusive household. That fleeting freedom she enjoyed out of the home of her parents would, however, come with consequences, for my mother had already fallen in love with intensity and excitement, and at every opportunity would create high drama as a way of feeling alive. Not surprisingly, such an attitude meant that she was not cut out for the humdrum of domesticity and routine. As soon as the household was on an even keel, she'd find a way to rock the boat.

My mother gave birth to me a year after the wedding, in 1926, when she was only fifteen years old. My given name was Marie, but everyone except my grandmother called me Mary. As the first child, I was the center of attention and my father's pride and joy, and as a little girl, I remember feeling safe when he held me in his arms. The family grew bigger. My brother, Larry, was born in 1928 and my brother, Carmine, in 1932. Then, in 1933, came my sister, Fran. And last was the baby, Peter, who was born in 1937. A sixth child, who was stillborn with a broken spine and weighed more than thirteen pounds, would have been named Victor if he'd lived.

We inhabited a gray, semi-detached, two-family house on Shore Avenue. Because it was a cul-de-sac, the street was like its own little community. Everyone was in everyone else's business. You grew up playing and making friends with people on your block.

My best friend growing up was Helen Dragone, who lived at the end of the street. Helen and her parents had emigrated from Italy when she was seven years old, and she'd nearly starved. Like me, she was the eldest child in an Italian family, which meant she was responsible for helping her mother take care of the house. We were both given duties way beyond our chronological age, and we'd help each other out long after we'd grown up.

The neighborhood contained everything you needed. The doctor's office, the drug store, and the deli were just around the corner. At the grocery store, Irving Cohen would write down in a book behind the counter what you owed, and you paid up at the end of the week. That's what business was like back then. If you wanted entertainment, you could go the Plaza Theatre, located the next block over on 150th Avenue. With six-hundred seats and a single screen, it showed movies like *The Best Years of Our Lives* and *The Big Sleep*. The theater was directly behind our house, so it was like having Dana Andrews, Myrna Loy, Humphrey Bogart, and Lauren Bacall in our backyard.

Very few people owned cars. We had no telephone or oil heating. The house was warmed by coal, which was stored in the basement. The stove in the kitchen was used for both cooking and heat. My father cut a hole in the kitchen wall and put in a panel that could be removed in the winter to let the heat pass through into the front room.

The basement was where my father made his own cheese and the stink of it would waft up the stairs. He also brewed his own wine in barrels down there. Many of the neighbors did this too, in secret. The Prohibition Era only ended in 1933, and the neighborhood's scrappy entrepreneurialism more than once tipped into breaking the law, or at least, bending it. A story from those times went that, one day, word spread that inspectors were coming around. My father lugged the wine barrels up from the basement and rolled them out the back door. He rolled them right through a hole in the fence that he'd cut especially for that purpose and into the neighbor's backyard. When the inspectors arrived at the house next door, the neighbor used the same hole to roll his wine barrels into our yard. Neither man was caught, nor a single barrel lost.

Every day, my father took the bus to Queens Village where he loaded trucks for Borden Dairy. Because his job was steady, he was always able to provide for us, even during the Depression. At the very least, our house was supplied with milk. When my father arrived home after work, he'd reach for the bottle of homemade wine by the table and drink for the whole evening. Somehow, he'd be sober by morning and ready for another day's work.

In general, when he wasn't drinking, my father was a good man. He supported a large family. He loved his wine-and-cheese making. He enjoyed taking care of the tomato plants and fig trees he grew in the backyard. In the winter, he would borrow one of our coats to cover a fig tree like it was one of his children. But when he was drinking, my father would become a monster, especially toward my mother. He wouldn't just hit her, but he'd throw her across the room and smash her against the wall. He was jealous of her because she was so beautiful and much younger than him. He always thought she was cheating on him.

"I saw you!" he'd yell. His face, already red from drinking, would burn even redder. "I saw you talking to him!" This would be about a storeowner or a neighbor. Or just a stranger walking down the street.

"I didn't talk to anybody," my mother would chirp. She was unable to keep from talking back even if it was in her best interest to keep silent—because then he'd really slug her. My response, as the eldest, and almost preternaturally aware of my need to protect my siblings and try to establish order and peace, was to separate my parents when they were fighting. As a child of nine or ten, I would shut my mother up in another room, where her mouth and even just the sight of her face wouldn't set my father off.

Once, I wasn't able to act fast enough and could only bundle the other kids upstairs so they were out of the way. My father was incandescent with rage at my mother—I didn't know over what, but probably the usual. "You were too friendly. You're cheating on me." The walls shook with his shouting and the pounding of his fists. Every time a blow landed; I could feel the impact like it was on my own body. I looked at my brother, Larry. From the expression on his face, it seemed like he could feel it too.

Growing up in this atmosphere of violence would mark me for the rest of my life. It's a condition that affects many children of alcoholics or those who are raised in families where the borders between adult and child, between the dangerous outside world and the safety of a warm and loving home, are porous or have broken down altogether. I squelched the natural exuberance of the child, and became hyper-responsible. I was as guarded as my mother was emotionally excessive, and as calm and even accepting as my father was volatile and jealous. I rarely joked, played, or had fun. I cultivated a tough exterior—tougher than I actually was, probably. Such a premature adulthood would influence my relationships with men, especially my husband. Larry told me he hated our father and could never forgive him for hitting our mother. It took me many, many years before I could forgive my father too.

My mother just wasn't equipped to stand up for herself. In fact, it became obvious within a few years of marriage that she wasn't equipped to be a mother. Certainly, she made sure that we were clothed and had food to eat, but she was not a nurturing woman whom you could trust with your innermost thoughts. She'd married so young, and had started having children when still only in her mid-teens, that she essentially never grew up. Flighty, easily distractible, and prone to pouting and sulking, my mother never asked us about our day in school or whether we'd finished our homework. My mother also loved to gossip and complain about her life, her husband, and everyone else on the block. These characteristics weren't something that any of us ever blamed her for. After all, you can't give what you don't have. But as a result, I found myself taking on more and more tasks on behalf of the family. When my brothers fell into trouble at school, it was I who'd talk to their teachers. On cold nights, I would heap coats over the blankets to keep my siblings warm, like they were my father's fig trees.

Although a cross hung on the kitchen wall, there wasn't much of a presence of God at home. My parents never entered a church except on the holidays. Unlike other kids in the neighborhood, my siblings and I didn't attend Catholic School. But we did learn the catechism, and we received our communion and confirmation.

When I was seven years old, I received my first Holy Communion. I woke up that cold and rainy morning, excited to get dressed for the occasion. "Bella," my grandmother cooed, as she tied the sash at the waist of my white dress. I looked at my grandmother and thought she was beautiful too, with her dark red hair that my mother and later, my sister, Fran, inherited.

My grandmother, my parents, my little brothers, and I walked to church together. I was young enough to be excited about being in front of the congregation and the center of attention. But I was also old enough to know that when the communion wafer was placed on my tongue, it was the body of Christ. The sip of wine was the blood of Christ. I believed this with my head, but not with my heart.

After I returned from church, I needed to be by myself. I walked out on the porch. I could sense behind me the warm inside of the house, with my parents and brothers talking. But instead of feeling alone, I sensed very intensely and surely that God was with me. Something was happening to me. This was the first time that the feeling that washed over me in church—that encompassing sense of joy—spread outside to my life at home. I began to understand how it could be possible to have God always by your side. The joy didn't have anything to do with what was hanging on the wall or even the words you spoke. It had to do with the spirit within.

I was beginning to understand what my grandmother was trying to give me by taking me to church all those mornings while I was growing up.

My grandmother always stood up for me. I was a skinny child and everyone thought I was sickly. People would try to make me eat, but my grandmother would say, "Marie is fine, leave her alone."

Like many first-born children in a dysfunctional or addicted household, I worked hard to keep the peace between my parents, whose essential incompatibility beyond their immediate physical attraction became more and more evident—and not just to me. When I was nine years old, I started working at a dry-goods store in the neighborhood owned by a Jewish family, the Kapps, who wanted to adopt me. They could see that I was intelligent, hard-working, and had potential, and they were aware of trouble in our home. They approached my family and offered to take me in. My father refused categorically. He loved me and was proud of me; I was his first-born after all. But, at least, part of his calculation in refusing the offer was that I was essential to the family: I brought in money through my job, I looked after my siblings in the absence or negligence of my mother, and I kept the household functioning to my father's satisfaction. In essence, I became the wife that he didn't have.

It's hard to imagine such a situation in the United States today, and yet, among poor immigrant families, it wasn't unusual for families to be broken up and children sent to relatives, orphanages, or adopted out, should there not be enough money to look after all of the children. I myself was torn: the Jewish family was orderly, supportive, and I knew they loved me and that they would present me with opportunities and chances to flourish in a way that my own family wouldn't or couldn't. Nonetheless, I cared deeply about my siblings, and even at the age of nine, I assumed a great deal of responsibility for them.

During these years, the church was a lifeline, as it had been to my grandmother. A place of solace, peace, and reflection, it offered me a sanctuary from the craziness of my family, where I could be myself and not the adult-child I was forced to be at home. I loved the rituals, candles, and the fostering of the imagination and the release from drudgery that the physical space of the church offered me. I realize now that part of my attraction to the church as a child was because it was associated with my grandmother's love. With her, I was freed from the obligations of being a dutiful daughter who kept the peace and was someone my father could rely on–even, or especially, when he was drunk. I could be a child again, one who was the focus of an unconditional love that was grounded in family and faith. Thankfully, while my brothers didn't care very much about religion, my sister, Fran, became quite devout, and so we shared that connection, as well as a bedroom.

Then, when I was twelve years old, my grandmother died. She'd had a heart attack. The one person who truly understood me was gone.

The night before the funeral was the wake. According to tradition, one person was supposed to stay in the same room with the body overnight. My parents decided that because I'd been so close to my grandmother, that person would be me. Overwhelmed by loss, I sat in a chair all night next to my grandmother's cold, lifeless form. I struggled to stay awake by remembering how warm her hands were, holding mine as we walked into church, and wondering just who would look out for me now that she was dead. Without my grandmother, a light had been extinguished that even God couldn't bring back.

Looking back, I can see how the church that my grandmother and I attended together became a physical and psychological space where I could express wonder and awe and feel surrounded by affection. It's not surprising, therefore, that the kind of religious experience that I had on the porch was an intimacy with God, and it's also not surprising how easily that dissipated, as I sat beside the cold body of my loving grandmother. The church, and by extension, the church was a fairyland retreat, and my grandmother, my fairy godmother. Both were fantasies necessary for my survival—but fantasies nonetheless.

A year later, when I was thirteen, I received confirmation. I entered this process without much pleasure. I was very lonely. *What's to become of me?* I thought. Without my grandmother, I didn't have anyone. This time, I understood the seriousness of the sacrament. Receiving confirmation would bind me to the church and enrich me with the gifts of the Holy Spirit. As a true witness of Christ, I would be obliged to spread and defend the faith by word and deed.

Was I ready to make this commitment?

I considered this as I kneeled before the bishop in his red robes underneath the ceiling of St. Pius. He anointed my forehead in the sign of the cross with the holy chrism of oil.

"Be sealed with the gift of the Holy Spirit."

He wiped away the oil and held his hands over me.

"May the Holy Spirit enter your soul."

I realized what these words truly meant. The Holy Spirit was now a part of me—I had accepted God into my life and there He would remain for the rest of my days. He would give me the strength to spread His teachings to those who needed it, especially if I was the one who needed it the most. I knew this with as much certainty as my eyes saw or my heart beat.

Confirmation was one of the most sacred vows of my life, and the beginning of my true relationship with God. One morning, while sitting at the kitchen table, I announced to my family that I wanted to become a nun.

"You do that," my mother returned, laughing. "You should continue to plan on becoming a nun."

My mother glanced at my siblings at the table. Larry and Carmine started laughing too. Even Fran, who was only four years old and probably didn't understand exactly what being a nun meant, began to giggle. Instead of recognizing in me a child grieving the loss of the one person who understood her religious impulses, and looking to provide consolation or, indeed, the strengthening in one's faith that is the purpose of the sacrament of confirmation, my mother joined with my siblings in mocking me. I looked around at all those laughing faces, pushed back my chair, and walked out to my usual refuge, the porch. I missed my grandmother more than ever.

* * *

The burdens of taking care of the family only increased as I grew older, and more and more my thoughts turned to escape. But getting out of Jamaica, Queens, was not that easy. Despite some of the idyllic, small-town qualities of the neighborhood, once you grew into a teenager, there were plenty of bad roads you could take. Many young people dropped out of school and turned to drugs. Heroin, which began to flood the working-class neighborhoods of New York City in the latter 1940s, was the drug of choice, and the addiction and criminality it brought with it would later affect my family, as it did many others. For boys, one option was joining the army, which my brothers, Larry and Carmine, eventually did. Things were harder if you were a girl.

Maybe education would be my way out, I thought. I was a very good student, especially in French. Since becoming a nun was becoming less and less practical an option for me, I decided that I wanted to become a nurse.

This dream too, came crashing down.

At age seventeen, and about to enter my senior year in high school, my father informed me I would not be attending school anymore.

"We need to save money for Larry to go to school," he announced. "Besides, a girl doesn't need an education."

I thought of the Kapps, and wondered whether they would have made the same decision.

As harsh as my father's judgment was, it was not uncommon during that time. People thought an education was wasted on a girl because she would get married and become a housewife. Until she met her husband, she should work to help bring money into the family.

Although I minded not being able to graduate from high school, I wasn't sorry to leave Jamaica High, which Larry and I both went to. The demographics of the neighborhood were changing, and the students were mostly African American—Larry was the only white kid in his class. In our highly balkanized yet densely populated communities—the Italians with the Italians, the Poles with the Poles, the Irish with the Irish, the African Americans with their own—an enforced co-existence who demarcated by which street corner you stood on, which roads you walked on, and where you traced your roots from. All communities had their prejudices, their strivers, and their ne'er-do-wells, and my community was no different.

I know there's a tendency for inner-city folks in all ethnic groups to look back on their youth in the 1930s and 1940s and remember only stickball in the streets, *Little Rascals*, open backdoors, and neighbors looking out for each other. But life was very tough: not only through the

Depression, when many men lost their jobs, but through World War II, when those same men marched off to fight and returned home, some of them with what we'd now call PTSD. Organized crime, turf wars, loan sharks, and gang fights also scarred our blocks. In our neighborhood, even walking to school posed dangers, since you had to pass by the railroad tracks where dangerous men loitered. A girl could get raped, or worse. Later, my parents wised up and used an uncle's address to send the other kids to a better high school.

Since my only option was to work, I landed a job at Gertz Department Store on Jamaica Avenue. Started by Benjamin Gertz in 1918 as a stationery store, Gertz became one of the biggest independent department stores in New York City, rivaling Macy's. I worked my way up (literally), from skirts on the third floor to fine china on the sixth. All those beautifully made tea sets and crystal instilled in me a taste for nice things that I was never to lose. The entire family received a twenty-percent store discount, and I was later able to obtain for Larry an after-school job at the store as a window dresser, so my father was pleased. I was happy as well. I was a good saleswoman, and I liked my coworkers.

From the first day I met her on the sales floor, I could tell Helen Martin would be a great friend. With fair Irish skin, blue eyes, and black hair, Helen was statuesque and stunningly beautiful. She was eight years older than me and divorced from her ex-husband, a cop—shocking, since divorce was unusual for Catholics at the time. Helen was a motherly type, and the both of us shared a love for culture and a thirst for knowledge. I was also close to other coworkers, such as my friend, Mary Ehmer, but Helen was the one who would end up changing my life in a profound way.

In 1945, the war ended and America was starting to rebuild. At this point, to anyone in the neighborhood, it looked like I was well on the path of what was expected for a young woman about to enter her twenties. I would work until I married and set up my own household and then start to have babies. What neither my neighbors nor I could have foreseen, was the difficulties that such a life would present.

2 Magic

It was Friday evening, and I was sitting in front of the mirror, getting ready for a date. With charcoal, I penciled in my brows–in those days, we shaved the entire brow in order to achieve the proper arch. I powdered my face and added bright red lipstick. Then, I stood up and checked the rest of my appearance. I was petite but the belted-in waist of my red dress showed off what I would later call my Elizabeth Taylor figure. In those days, I wanted to look more like Loretta Young, though. After all, my middle name was Loretta.

It had been difficult to keep up with fashions during the war; yet, a year or so after it ended, women had more choices than ever. *Vogue* and *Charm* magazines featured models in sharp suits and with slim silhouettes. Although I wasn't about to riot for the chance to wear nylon stockings, I liked taking care of how I looked. Fortunately, I was handy with sewing, and after work I could visit the 'Young Elegant Shop' on the third floor at Gertz, to see what latest styles I could copy. I wanted to look as attractive as possible this evening.

My little sister, Fran, followed me as I walked out of the bedroom we shared.

"What are you doing?" I asked.

"I'm going with you," she replied.

"On my date?"

"Mom told me to."

With an exasperated sigh, I walked downstairs and opened the door for my date—Joseph Mrozowski.

I'd always had plenty of suitors; they'd line up at my front door, waiting to knock. One was a young professor who let me know he was madly in love with me. But Joe was special. Tall and handsome, he had the same brooding, heavy-lidded, passive, and yet, slightly dangerous quality that I associate with the actor, Robert Mitchum, except he had blond hair and blue eyes. Everywhere he went, girls would turn their heads to look at him. He made my heart flutter—if I may say so, he made *more* than my heart flutter, and we had an undeniable physical attraction for one another. Everyone who knew us could see it. One of my classmates wrote in my graduation yearbook, *"Mary and Joe sitting in a tree, K-I-S-S-I-N-G. First comes love, then comes marriage, then comes baby in a baby carriage."*

I guess my mother could see it, too—not least for the obvious reason that I was about to follow in her footsteps.

I'd met Joe when I was fifteen, not much older than my mother was when she met my father. Maybe that was why she was making Fran tag along on our dates. When we arrived home, my mother would ask Fran where Joe and I had been sitting, what we'd been doing—not censoriously, but in an annoyingly gossipy manner, rather like a friend quizzing you. Of course, the answer would be 'nothing.' I wasn't about to make the same mistake my mother had by committing myself too soon. Joe and I hung out on the corner or we went to the movies. Sometimes, we headed to Far Rockaway Beach and Jones Beach. In our swimsuits, we looked like a couple straight out of the movies.

Joe was four years older than me and lived on Liberty Avenue, which was just a couple of blocks away. The fourth of six sons, he hung out with his older brother, Chester, and was the favorite of his mother, Paulette. He even slept in the same bed as Paulette until he was fourteen. Once, Joe casually let on to me that he used to squeeze his mother's nipples, which I found ridiculous and bizarre, although, perhaps I should have been more alarmed at what this presaged about what he expected from a marital bond. I never saw her smile, and I couldn't understand her because she only spoke Polish.

Joe's father had died when he was a child. Because of that, the family met with great difficulties during the Depression. Often, they didn't have enough to eat, which forever implanted in Joe a sense of deprivation. He valued hard work and was a salesman for Baker's Restaurant Equipment, selling stoves, refrigerators, dishwashers, and small sundries like plates and utensils. The company serviced well-known restaurants throughout Manhattan and on Long Island. It was Jewish-owned and Joe often complained that his salary was too low—anti-Semitism wasn't unusual during this time, or in this Polish community.

Joe and I were constantly breaking up and getting back together. Joe was always flirting with other girls, and doing goodness knows what else. I was twenty-one when we married, and I entered that estate as a pragmatist. Joe and I had already had sex, but I was sufficiently a traditionalist that it never occurred to me that I wouldn't then marry him. I recognized that our mutual attraction might not last, but I fervently hoped that we might at least be committed to one another, with shared values and a meeting of minds.

At our wedding, I wore a lilac suit and a hat decorated with a veil and an ostrich feather. I had made the hat myself, since I'd once worked in a millinery. My father didn't like my casual outfit, but I didn't care; nor did I mind that the wedding reception was small. What was important to me was that the ceremony be a Nuptial Mass, with all of the proper rites. I insisted on that because I considered marriage to be a sacrament and a holy vow. I looked on religion as something like magic, and God as the ultimate magician. *Say a novena and your wish will be granted. Just pray and all will be well.*

I prayed that my marriage would be perfect.

After the wedding, I moved out of the house on Shore Avenue and with Joe into his mother's house for the longest six months of my life. Maybe Joe's childhood sleeping arrangements should have tipped me off, but it wasn't long before I realized something was wrong with Paulette's mind. She was never formally diagnosed, but I think she had some form of mental illness, possibly paranoia. At times, she'd confuse Joe with her dead husband. She'd stare at me, eyes fixated on my every move, and say nothing.

One day, I returned home from work to hear Joe and his mother arguing in the living room.

"What's she saying?" I asked Joe.

Reluctantly, Joe translated, "You steal her things."

I laughed at the idea that anything Paulette owned was worth taking.

This seemed to make Paulette even angrier and she hissed something that sounded like a curse.

"She says that you stole her son too."

She meant Joe. In that moment, I realized I had to put my foot down. I turned to Joe, "We have to leave, right now."

"But—" he stammered.

I pointed toward Paulette, "It's either her or me."

That night, Joe and I returned to my parents' house on Shore Avenue. We couldn't stay any other place. For a year, we slept on a mattress in the living room, saving up enough to get our own place. My parents didn't mind because they liked Joe. Everyone in my family did—they thought he was quiet and nice.

Finally, Joe and I bought our own place in Baisley Park, a Queens's neighborhood a few miles south of Jamaica. The house was small, with two bedrooms and a tiny backyard, but it was all ours. I loved decorating it, especially the dining area, since I was able to display the fine Blue Willow china, I'd purchased from Gertz. One set had a cobalt blue-and-white castle scene, a pattern that was designed in England, although these pieces had been made by Buffalo Pottery in Buffalo, New York. Another set, a light gray bone china with delicate rosebuds, was stamped 'Occupied Japan.' I matched the china with a maroon rug, the color combination producing a stunning effect.

Our new house was near Woodrow Wilson High School, which Fran attended. She'd stop by after school and tell me what was happening in the old neighborhood. Even though I'd had my issues with my sister, especially when we were sharing a room growing up, I was glad now to have her around. In fact, several years later when Fran married, she and her husband, Al, moved into the Baisley Park house with Joe and me. I was glad to offer them a place because I remembered what it was like to be newlyweds without a home of one's own. I even gave Fran our bedroom and insisted that Joe and I sleep in the basement. Fran and Al lived with us for a year.

Although our living situation had improved, those early years of marriage were difficult for Joe and me. Joe was often away at work, and when he was home, he'd complain about money, despite the fact that I was working as hard as he was. I was making an effort, but I sank into despondency. Emptiness gnawed away at me, a sense that marriage was not what I'd thought it would be. As I always like to say, if you want to suffer, have expectations.

Starting a family, I believed, would help allay some of my unease with my marriage. At first, Joe didn't want to have kids, but he could see how much children meant to me. And children *did* mean everything to me. All the babies I'd held when I visited the poor immigrant families with my mother; my siblings, whom I'd practically raised on my own because our mother was so incompetent: I was deeply attached to that aspect of caregiving. Life—and God—couldn't be that cruel to deny me what I so desperately wanted.

When I was twenty-four, I thought I might finally be pregnant. My stomach began to rise until it looked like I was a few months along. Full of hope, I visited the doctor, expecting him to tell me that my greatest wish had been granted.

"I'm sorry, Mrs. Mrozowski," the doctor said. "There is no baby. What you have is a tumor."

I was in complete shock. Instead of bearing life inside me, I was carrying something dark and dangerous that could kill me. The doctor explained to me that I needed an operation, and without knowing much more about my condition, I agreed with his diagnosis. The tumor was removed, along with my ovaries. Not only had major parts of my body been taken from me, but so had my hopes of bearing biological children. Later, I learned that the doctor who'd cut me up had the reputation of being a drug addict. Most likely, he'd been stoned while he operated on me. Did I receive the correct diagnosis? I would never know.

My body physically recovered, but mentally, I was in a bad place. Would I ever have a baby? A child to call my own? Even though it wasn't true, I'd believed myself to be pregnant. I had imagined a little girl dressed in a white christening gown, and now she was gone. I prayed and prayed to St. Jude, the saint of the impossible. *Oh, St. Jude, help me.*

Joe understood how devastated I was and agreed that we should put in an application at the Catholic Home Bureau to adopt. Not everyone thought this was a good idea. My father, for instance, thought we were crazy. "Why would you want someone else's troubles?" he asked.

While we were waiting for our application to come through, my friend, Helen Martin, informed me that she had learned of a pregnant woman who needed a place to stay. The woman was a few months along, and if Joe and I agreed to host her for the rest of her pregnancy, we could have the baby when it was born. This would be an independent adoption, sometimes informally called a 'gray adoption,' meaning one that takes place outside of an agency or formal organization. We made sure we had an attorney in case something went wrong.

I gleaned some information about the biological mother. Her family name was Italian, like my own. Like me, she had long, black hair, although she was significantly taller at 5'8". She was twenty-nine years old and was afraid of telling her father and brothers in Brooklyn that she was pregnant. The biological father was Irish, and her father didn't like him.

We agreed to the transaction, and the biological mother moved into the Baisley Park house with Joe and me. I made sure that she ate properly and was well-rested. Although I didn't exactly keep her a secret from my friends and family, I refused to allow anyone to come to the house and visit me while she was there. I didn't want the biological mother to develop a relationship with my family and someday try to reach the baby through them. I wanted to ensure that no one could take my child away from me.

My first daughter was born on March 9, 1952. Her homecoming day—the day we were allowed to take her home—was March 17. I named her Judith Thadine, after St. Jude, who had made the impossible, possible, and the Hebrew word for 'given praise.' The biological mother was in the hospital for seven days, not because the birth had been complicated, but because she wanted to be with the baby and couldn't let go. After she was discharged, however, she fled to Massachusetts with the father and no one was able to find her for the next two years. It was torture not knowing whether she'd come back and whisk the baby from me, and

I prayed day and night against this possibility. At one point, my lawyer informed me that the biological mother wanted the baby back and had refused to sign the surrender papers. A Jewish family was offering her $10,000 for the baby. But in the end, she agreed to give Judith to me. It must have been difficult for her to let go of her baby, but it was an act of love on her part. She discerned it would be disruptive for Judith after spending the first two years of her life with me.

Some people would say that Judith was adopted by accident. If Helen Martin hadn't found out about this pregnant woman who needed a place to hide from her Italian family, Judith wouldn't be my daughter. I don't see it that way. I take Helen's suggestion as a sign from God and St. Jude. It was a miracle that God would allow me to be the mother of this beautiful child. Now, when I worshipped in church, my prayer life had an increased intensity. During the time I'd been praying to St. Jude for a baby, I'd joined the Legion of Mary, and now, I wanted to be of more service. I wanted to visit poor people in my neighborhood, just as my grandmother and I had when I was growing up. So, with baby Judith, I attended evening prayer vigils that were full of lighted candles, processions, and singing. These rituals provided me with as much joy as they had when I was a child.

Once Judith became legally mine, and there was no chance the biological mother could return and remove her from me, I wanted to be closer to my family. Joe and I sold the Baisley Park house and bought one attached to my parents' on Shore Avenue. Meanwhile, our original application with the Catholic Home Bureau was still churning through the system. Some two and a half years after Judith was born, the Bureau told us that they had a baby for us: another little girl, a sister for Judith. She was six months old at the time. The biological parents were unmarried college students, and the biological mother's father was a powerful exporter who demanded that she surrender her child for adoption. The mother was from a Portuguese and Finnish background and was Catholic, while the father was from a Swedish background and Protestant, so there must have been a religious conflict.

The baby's birth name was Charlotte Ann, which I changed to Janet Theresa—I wanted both girls to have names that started with the same initial as their father's. Blond and blue-eyed, Janet had something of Joe's coloring. Next to a darker-haired, green-eyed Judith, it was hard to believe the two were sisters. On October 15, 1955, Janet's homecoming day, I put Janet in Judith's arms. "This is *your* gift," I told her. Judith looked up at me as if she'd received the best present in the world.

From the beginning, my daughters were aware that they were adopted. I explained to them they'd been 'chosen,' as indeed I believed to be the case. The entrance of my children into my life was the greatest turning point I could have expected, and turned me into a complete woman. My children's lives have brought me more gifts than any human being on earth. I can never express how thankful I was for them.

Living in Jamaica, Queens, Judith and Janet saw what it was like when I was growing up. In spite of the changing dynamics and a host of other social upheavals in the city, the neighborhood hadn't changed much, and many of the same families lived on the block. At night, everyone would come out on their porches and mingle with one another, catching up on gossip. My best friend, Helen Dragone, gave birth to a girl six months before Judith was born. Helen looked to me for advice on how to take care of her baby. Her daughter, Antoinette, and Judith grew up together and became good friends. They'd ride their bikes from one end of the street to the other, attend birthday parties together, and practically lived at each other's house.

Joe, always looking for new business ventures, decided that we should buy a hardware store around the corner on Sutphin Boulevard. We stocked it with not only tools, but general supplies, such as stationery, cookware, and baby-dolls, which we gave to the girls as presents for Christmas. With my sales skills from Gertz, I ran the place efficiently.

When Judith was four years old, I placed her in daycare so I could oversee the store while taking care of Janet. Janet would sit beside me in the back of the store as I reconciled the bills or tended to customers. Because she'd spent six months in foster care, Janet was very quiet and observant. I often wondered whether she'd received much attention in that foster home and if that family ever held her, since she tended to stay in one place and not move a lot. She was, however, excited to see Judith when she came home, smiling and grabbing at her to play.

The daycare that Judith attended was at St. Joseph's Church and run by the Josephite nuns, who were known for being strict. Joe would pick up Judith after work and tell me the kids were lying in cots waiting for their parents. When Judith saw Joe, she was overwhelmed with excitement to go home. Later, we sent Judith to kindergarten, and first and second grade, with the Josephite nuns. I was sure they'd give her a good education, even if they were severe.

With the hardware store, we were bringing in good money. Joe was doing well at his job and was finally receiving a higher salary. After five years back in Jamaica, we did what many families in the city did, which was to move to the suburbs on Long Island. Jamaica was starting to become an even tougher neighborhood, with drugs on the street, and the children couldn't play outdoors anymore without adult supervision.

Plainview, Oyster Bay, was located mid-island, about an hour's drive from Manhattan. Originally a town inhabited by fruit farmers, by the late 1950s, many Italian and Jewish families had moved there from the city. It was a safe community dotted with shopping centers and farm stands, and a few churches and synagogues. Most of the houses were Cape Cods or split-levels and stood along tree-lined streets. The children could walk safely to the local schools, which were considered quite good.

We were welcomed as soon as we moved onto Birch Drive. The next block over, on Wallace Drive, lived two families whom I grew to know well. One was the Dalools— Mary was Italian and Albert was Lebanese—and they had three children. The other was Angelo and Connie Silveri, a newly married couple who would become like family, and later became my dearest friends and benefactors, helping me more than I can ever say.

Our house was a white Cape Cod with dormer windows and black shutters. Because it was the last house on a dead-end street, it was very private. The property covered several acres and used to be part of a farm—the two-car garage had an attached barn. Strawberry patches, and apple and pear orchards, still grew on the land. Later, New York State Route 135, which ran north to south and connected the Long Island Expressway to the Southern State Parkway, was built across our property. We were left with only one acre and were never reimbursed for the loss.

For the first time in my life I had a house larger than I knew what to do with. The first floor contained the living room, kitchen, and a small bedroom with a bathroom. The second floor had three bedrooms and a bathroom, so the girls could each have their own rooms. I enjoyed decorating each room and changed the colors of the bedding to match the seasons. Out was brought the fine china and we used it at every meal. On Sundays, I'd allow the girls to each choose a tea cup from my collection for a special breakfast. The garden, though, was my glory. I had a green thumb and loved to have something blooming during the growing season. I planted a daffodil bed in the back of the house and a bed of huge purple rhododendrons in the front. I was happiest when I worked in that garden.

Joe fancied himself a carpenter and built the children's dressers into the sloped walls of the front bedrooms. He fixed up the barn next to the garage and dug up the basement floor, saying it needed to be raised. As he was the kind of man who often started things but rarely finished them, I should have known better than to believe him.

Now that we had the space, I agreed to the girls' request for pets. Janet acquired a cat, which she named Lady. For her ninth birthday, we took Judith to a local shelter and adopted a mutt whom we named Sheba. Since our place used to be a farm, I thought it would be fun to have chickens to give us fresh eggs. The girls named our three chickens Jessie, Bessie, and Tessie. We had them for about a year, and then Joe asked his brother, Chester, who was a butcher, to come out from Queens. Chester cut off the chickens' heads, and the girls and I watched in horror as the bodies ran around afterward. This was hugely traumatic for Judith and Janet at the time, but, like many kids, they soon got over it.

Our family was complete for a while, but I couldn't help thinking of adding another child—a boy. I'd always wanted three children. Plus, I thought Joe might like a son. We decided to take in a foster child named Michael. The agency mentioned to us that he'd had some problems, as he'd been in many different foster homes, but when I looked at his scruffy brown hair and large dark eyes, all I could see was an innocent child who needed me. I truly believed that there wasn't anyone who couldn't be helped, especially a child.

I wanted to ensure my children had the best of everything. I was a skilled tailor and made them beautiful clothes. They had tutors for their schoolwork, music lessons—the violin, piano, guitar, accordion—and horseback-riding lessons. In the summer, I took them to Oyster Bay so they could learn how to swim. We'd visit my third cousins, who lived across the street from the beach at Theodore Roosevelt Memorial Park, and have picnics with them on the beach. I loved driving from Plainview to Oyster Bay, north on a winding road that passed through a scenic wooded area, where you could glimpse mansions between the trees. The children would pretend they were on a rollercoaster ride and shout with glee.

Mary Ehmer, my friend from Gertz, marveled about East Hampton and invited me to her vacation home on Squaw Road near the marina—the bay side where the working people lived. Eventually, a two-bedroom bungalow at the corner of the street became available, and with money my father willed to me, Joe and I bought it as a summer home. I looked on that second house as an investment, renting it out to a writer for nine months of the year, when the children were in school.

Summers in East Hampton were glorious. The house was less than a mile from the bay, and the children and I spent nearly every day on the beach. After a picnic lunch on a blanket, I made sure the children were covered in sunscreen and let them go play. I never exposed myself directly to the sun, as my skin was so fair. I remained under an umbrella while they spent hours digging for clams and picking small, pink-and-coral, pearl-like shells. At the end of the day, we'd return home with buckets of shells, sand in our bathing suits, and sea salt in our hair from the furious ocean.

On Saturday afternoons, I would take the children into town for their lessons. We'd stop at the secondhand clothing store stocked by castoffs from the wealthy people on the other side of town. One day, I found a pair of jodhpurs for Judith that had the name 'Jacqueline Bouvier' hand-embroidered in the lining of the pants. It was the nearest to living the life of the people who lived on the ocean side of East Hampton. In fact, on the way home, I'd drive past the mansions so that the children saw how the other half lived. I wanted them to remember their roots, but also to have high expectations for themselves.

Sometimes in the evening, we'd go to an outdoor movie at Hampton Drive-In on Montauk Highway. We'd watch the racing chariots from *Ben Hur* and desert armies from *Lawrence of Arabia* sweep across the larger-than-life screen. Driving back after the movie was challenging because the roads had no lights. I missed having Joe around on those nights.

If this life seems idyllic, then in many ways it was. If it seems too good to be true, then it was that as well. Beneath the outward signs of a comfortable and prosperous middle-class life, our family was under increasing amounts of stress. When Joe and I were together, it was clear that our physical attraction was as strong as ever. We didn't have to worry about birth control because I couldn't get pregnant, and so we were as intimate as often as we liked. It was like filling a jar with endless pennies. I recognized that a positive outlook on sex was important in a marriage, and Joe and I never had any difficulties on that front.

I was beginning, though, to have a problem with Joe's absence. In fact, I noticed that even when he was physically around, he seemed distracted or mentally not present. He didn't come to the house in East Hampton much. If he did, he'd spend the weekend fixing up the property, like digging a hole to build a cesspool. The hole grew bigger but nothing else was accomplished. We all fished in the bay once and returned with fresh blowfish for dinner. The children were happy whenever he was there, and so was I. While I was glad to have my friends on the street to socialize with, Joe's presence would have made life easier.

One Saturday, the girls decided they would take a walk down the road after dinner. I worried as the sky turned dark and they hadn't come home yet. Then I heard the backdoor close. I walked into the hall to see Judith and Janet with their arms full of fluffy cattails.

"Where were you?" I demanded.

Judith lifted up her bunch of cattails, "We saw a swamp and decided to pick these and bring them home."

"Wouldn't they make perfect brooms?" Janet added.

I could tell they were pleased with their find. Then, I noticed the tiny dark specks on their arms.

"What's that?" I bent closer and then screamed. "Ticks! You girls are covered in ticks!"

Judith and Janet screamed too.

I started picking the ticks off their skin. There must have been hundreds of them. Some of them were embedded and I had to use a lighter to get them out. *Why can't Joe be here to help me with this?* I wondered.

Aside from Joe being gone, though, I couldn't complain about much. We weren't quite at the level of the people who lived in those mansions tucked away from the road, but we were making a good living, owned two homes, and our lives were brightened by three children. Those years were truly some of the best years of my marriage and motherhood. Every day, I was surrounded by the magic of my family, carried on the crisp ocean breeze. The magic of God, who had fulfilled my very dreams.

Little did I know that this miraculous existence could be taken away from me so quickly.

3 Despair

In the kitchen of the house at Plainview, I could hear someone screaming from outside. The voice was thin, high-pitched, like a little girl's. Janet? I remembered that she and Michael were playing in the backyard.

I ran outside and followed the sound to the garage where Janet's cat, Lady, had recently given birth to a litter of kittens. Janet had helped delivered them herself and loved them dearly. Now, Janet looked at me with a tear-stained face, pointing through the glass-paned door of the garage. When I looked inside, I could see Michael standing over the bloody, crushed bodies of the kittens, a hammer in his hand. Janet had watched him kill them, helpless on the other side of the locked door. She was so distressed, she'd lost control of her bladder and bowels. I forced the door open to tend to Michael, leaving Janet to mourn and bury her beloved kittens.

This wasn't the first time Michael had shown violent behavior. Once, I'd been called to school because he'd kicked in a classroom door in a rage. The teacher had put Janet, who was in kindergarten at the time, in the same room with him, thinking his sister would be able to calm him down, but Janet was simply terrified.

Since Judith was older and bigger than he was, Michael didn't bother her. But he terrorized Janet. He'd draw scary pictures and chase her around the backyard. Fortunately, she was fast and agile, and could escape him by climbing into a tree. At night, when she couldn't get away from him, he'd sneak into her bedroom and stare at her in the dark. She'd awaken, so frightened that she'd go into Judith's room and beg to sleep with her or even on the floor. Since Joe and I slept downstairs, we never heard what was going on, and Janet was too scared to tell us. These days, parents would be much more vigilant about what their children were getting up to. But at the time, we assumed that most play was innocent.

Nonetheless, I was worried about his aggressive tendencies, and so began taking Michael to a psychiatrist. Judith and Janet would come with us and wait outside in the car during the hour-long sessions. The psychiatrist divulged to me that Michael was mentally ill and needed to be medicated. But I wasn't ready to give up on him. After the incident with the kittens, because Janet was so traumatized, I started taking her to Michael's psychiatrist as well. However, a year later, when Janet was only eight years old, Michael and a visiting cousin from Joe's side dragged her into the attic. While Michael held her down, the cousin prepared to sexually assault her. Janet broke away from them and screamed as loudly as she could. I ran upstairs and was furious when I found them; that cousin was never allowed to visit again. Janet began to have recurring nightmares.

Something had to change in our family situation, but too much else was occurring in my life for me to deal with it just yet. And so, to my great shame, I let things lie for the moment.

After Joe and I moved to Plainview, we still returned to my parents in Jamaica, Queens, every week for Sunday dinner. I looked forward to returning to the old neighborhood and seeing my siblings and their families. Fran and Al visited with their three daughters from Wantagh, Long Island. Peter, who was a firefighter, had married Carol, and they'd had two sons. He didn't have to travel far, as he lived across the street. After dinner, my father would take a nap on the couch while my siblings would talk and the cousins played together.

One Sunday evening, in the spring of 1961, my father didn't wake up. He was sixty-one when he passed away. The cause of death was determined to be cardiovascular hypertension. No one had any idea he was so sick. He'd only been in the hospital once in his adult life, for an ulcer. By this time, he'd cut down on his drinking and was so meek that the nurses didn't believe us when we explained that he used to be an abusive alcoholic. The year before he died, my father had been given a new job on the loading docks at Borden Dairy. The hard work had undoubtedly contributed to his poor health. He stopped enjoying the things that used to give him such pleasure. When Fran visited him in the early spring of that year, she noticed he hadn't dug up his beloved garden to plant the tomatoes.

When my father died, my mother finally had her life to herself—for a few years, at least. With her newfound sense of freedom, she did things she'd never had a chance to before, such as take a trip to Florida. While she was there, she was propositioned by a gentleman who wanted to 'shack up' with her—a euphemism that my mother laughed about and which I could tell she had no qualms about doing. I couldn't blame her: my mother was only in her early fifties and still beautiful.

My father left behind $16,000 in cash and the house. My siblings tried to grab the inheritance and split it up amongst themselves, but I didn't want any part of that. "It's our mother's money—let her spend it the way she wants to," I told them. It was as if time had been turned back and I had to make decisions for the family again. Except this time, I was the Doña, the one with the presence. My siblings did what I asked without questioning, at least to my face. As for me, I tried my best to be fair to everyone.

As it turns out, my mother ended up gambling away most of that inheritance. She had always been simple-minded about money. She was stupidly generous, giving you $500 if you asked for $250. Maybe she was making up for something she was missing in herself, like self-esteem. Even in her fifties, she retained her teenaged view of the world. She liked to make people laugh with her funny faces, and when I spent time with her, she enjoyed gossiping about her daughter-in-law to me as she braided Judith's hair. She also didn't pay any attention to her doctor's warning about her diabetes, which was getting worse.

Death seemed to be everywhere I turned. Not long after my father passed away, my good friend, Helen Martin, who'd led me to adopt Judith, died at age forty-six from open-heart surgery. She'd had the best doctor in the field, Dr. Michael DeBakey, who'd pioneered the procedure, but even he had been unable to save her. Tragically, a year later, her daughter, Patricia, also passed away, from a blood disease. Patricia had been a role-model for me growing up—a beautiful, educated girl who'd married a lawyer who was a Dartmouth graduate. She had two young children to whom she taught classical music and the arts, the same way I wanted to bring up my children.

Even more unexpected and tragic was the death of my cousin, Louis, in 1964. Cousin Lou was the adopted son of my mother's sister, Aunt Mary. He was close to me in age, and when we were young, he'd hang out at the house on Shore Avenue. For a time, he worked at Bella's Fruit Stand on Rockaway Boulevard in Jamaica. Later, he became a banker and married a woman who didn't like his family. We all thought his wife was an opportunist. When she found out Lou was adopted, she wanted to know who his biological family was, as if it had anything to do with her. Nobody in our family liked her—in fact, they hated her as much as they loved Lou.

One night, Lou had been working very hard and late. On his way home, he crashed his car into a concrete overpass on the Long Island Expressway. He died on impact.

I ended up not attending Lou's funeral or seeing the body laid out; it was too painful for me to reflect on yet another loss. I carried intense regret and shame over that. *Forgive me, Lord,* I pleaded. *Wipe away my sin and guilt. I surrender to you, O Lord, all of my beingness, my past and present.* I couldn't believe that the boy I'd spent so much time with as a girl was now dead. It was like something in my childhood had died as well. When would all these deaths end?

On a summer day, four years after my father's death, I received the call that my mother had suffered a heart attack and was in the hospital.

It was just Joe and me at home at the time, as the children were at Camp Auxilium in New Jersey. I'd started sending them to the camp, which was run by the Salesian Sisters of St. John Bosco, so they could get introduced to the spiritual life. They were due to come back soon, but I asked Joe to take them upstate to Howe Caverns, while I took care of my mother.

Every day for the next two weeks, I visited the hospital and sat by my mother's bedside. Small and weak, she looked more like a child than ever. She was only fifty-four years old, but I could see her time had come. I disclosed this to my siblings, and suggested that they should make peace with her, but they were in denial. My mother passed away on August 13, 1965. I was instantly plummeted into an all-encompassing grief. I hadn't felt this way since my grandmother's death when I was a child.

I'd been through so much grief that I simply couldn't bring myself to go to church anymore. Our church at the time was Our Lady of Mercy in Hicksville, where my children took catechism classes. I'd drop them off at the curb for Sunday Mass and pick them up, and then we'd go home to our special breakfast with tea, soft-boiled eggs, and pastries. Judith and Janet would tell me what happened at church that day, including how one of the ushers looked at them with unwelcoming eyes and escorted them out early because Michael couldn't sit still.

I started to have serious angina attacks from the stress and gained a great deal of weight, which affected how I looked and felt about myself. So, I did what a lot of people in the 1960s did to lose weight or get a rush. I started taking 'diet pills,' which were really 'uppers,' or amphetamines. While I was on them, my weight fell to 113 pounds. But the pills were highly addictive and made me manic and not present for my children.

I ignored the problematic side-effects of the pills as long as I grew thin. I came out of mourning (I'd been wearing only black for the past few years). For Mother's Day one year, Judith and Janet bought me a bright yellow-and-white housecoat as a gift. When I put it on, I could see their eyes shining with delight at how attractive I was. One night, when Joe took me to a party, I wore an elegant white silk dress decorated with red roses. My waist must have been twenty inches around. I hoped Joe would notice how nice I looked, but the morning after, he only accused me of flirting with another man.

My friend, Helen Dragone's husband, Henry Porretta, who never complimented anyone, always remarked to her, "Mary's so beautiful, she could have any man. Why did she marry that Joe?"

That was a good question. With all these deaths happening around me, I was ignoring the signs of what would become one of the biggest deaths in my life—the death of my marriage.

Things hadn't been good between Joe and me for a long time. For all his meekness, so unlike my own father's, Joe could also be volatile and jealous, and an unspoken anger always lingered. At such moments, the Robert Mitchum of the sleepy eyes became the Robert Mitchum of *The Night of the Hunter* or *Cape Fear*. As soon as the children had gone

73

to bed, the fireworks started exploding. It always began with some excuse, like Joe accusing me of not working enough or working too much. When I was angry, unlike my dramatic mother, I would become ice-cold: the timbre of my voice, drawn from the diaphragm, would deepen and darken, and my words would become clipped. "How. Dare. You," I'd say, my voice barely above a whisper. Inevitably, however, the argument would escalate until we were both screaming at each other and even throwing chairs around, waking the children.

Sometimes, Judith took Janet and Michael out of the house and down the block to our neighbors, the Dalools, to get away from it all. "I'm going to get you out of here," she'd tell them. "We'll run away. We'll go to my friend, Debi's house." Like the Kapps, the kindly family who'd expressed such an interest in me as a child, Debi's family, the Burtons, were Jewish and they too, offered a stable environment. It was clear I was repeating all of the mistakes with my own children that my own mother and father had made with me. Yet, few had any idea about our fights. Because we lived at the end of the street, the neighbors couldn't hear us. When Joe and my marriage ended, everyone was shocked because on the outside, it seemed like we were the perfect couple. Inside, we were being torn apart by our arguments.

Joe and I argued about everything and anything. He was particularly bothered by my faith and didn't like me telling the children that there was a heaven and a god.

"Don't put your religiosity onto them," he'd say.

"Joe," I'd reply, "this was the way I was brought up. It's important for them to know about the church."

"Mark my words, Mary, this is the beginning of the end."

It was, although I didn't know it yet.

As usual, money was a constant source of conflict. Joe was, in a word, cheap. He'd grown up amid scarcity, and, although I'm relieved he didn't compensate for that deprivation with unnecessary extravagance, he nonetheless didn't like me spending money. I'll admit I liked things like well-made clothes and fine china, but the money I spent was my own. When we moved to Plainview, I became a representative for Tupperware. In the mid-1950s, Tupperware parties were all the rage, and I enjoyed inviting groups of people over to my house.

I performed especially well and quickly climbed the corporate ladder. An opportunity arose for Joe and me to go into the business as a couple, but Joe didn't want to have anything to do with it. We could have made quite a lot of money, and I was disheartened when he turned the chance down.

On top of those businesses, I worked the night shift as a waitress at a local joint called the Cadillac Diner. During that time, Joe would be at home sleeping, so we barely saw each other.

One winter day, I called Joe to come pick me up after my shift ended at the diner. A snowstorm was brewing, and I wanted to get home before the weather became too bad.

"You're on your own," Joe announced over the phone.

"What do you mean?" I asked, looking out the diner window at the snow falling thicker and faster. "You need to come get me."

"Why don't you ask your boss to take you home?" Joe abruptly hung up.

It dawned on me that Joe thought I was having an affair with my manager. This was ridiculous, but I knew he wouldn't listen if I tried to call back and explain. I could do nothing but pull on my boots and head out into the howling wind and snow. I walked home two miles in that blizzard. The snow was so deep that I sank into it over my knees.

Ironically, Joe was the one having an affair.

Her name was Louise. She possessed full lips and blond hair that was always teased into an updo. She was five years older than Joe, with four kids from her previous husband, an alcoholic—and she must have offered Joe the kind of adoring affection that he'd received from his mother, because she was already a grandmother! Louise worked in the coat department at Alexander's Department Store, another one of New York City's venerable establishments. Of course, she was a working woman with a steady job— Joe wouldn't have stood for it otherwise.

From the beginning, Louise was no secret from me. When Joe and I argued, the biggest insult I could come up with was to say to him, "You're not a man!" To which he would retort, "Then ask Louise!" I didn't want to ask Louise. I didn't want to know anything more about her.

When I first found out about the affair, I needed to talk to someone. I called my sister, Fran, and asked her what I should do.

Fran demurred, "I'm sorry, Mary. You either have to put it out of your mind, or leave him."

"How can I leave him?" I asked. "Catholics don't get separated or divorced."

"That's true," Fran agreed.

"I don't understand why this is happening," I complained. "Joe's never strayed before…"

"Well…"

I could tell that Fran had more information than she was willing to divulge. Maybe her husband, Al, had revealed something to her. While Fran and Al had been living with us in Baisley Park the first year they were married, Al and Joe had become good friends. Later, I found out that Al had been in the bar with Joe when he'd first met Louise.

"What is it?" I asked my sister. "Please tell me."

Fran admitted that she thought Joe might have had other affairs, as far back as when we were first married. There'd been a neighbor of ours, who was only a teenager when she'd begun babysitting for us. If this was true, Joe would have been twenty-five. I will admit that I'd heard rumors; in fact, they'd been one reason why Joe and I had moved out of Queens. Yet, I still found the thought of Joe carrying on with a teenager upsetting—an unfortunate reminder of my own father who had, effectively, been doing the same with my mother. It's evident to me looking back that all of Joe's jealousy toward me and his accusations that I was having affairs were aspects of the displacement of his guilt about his own.

Yet, for all the dysfunctional marriages I'd endured— my parents' and my own—I didn't want to end mine. I used to tell my children that I could live with the Devil. Furthermore, I'd good reasons not to break up the marriage: I'd taken a vow before God when I married Joe; I'd prayed for children, and their care was a privilege and a sacred promise. I considered these children a gift from God, and adoption, I believed, carried even more of a burden of fidelity.

In the fall of 1965, Joe moved out of the house. Even then I was in denial. *Okay*, I thought to myself. *He's just angry. He'll come to his senses and return in time for Christmas. He has to spend Christmas with the children.*

Christmas had always been a major event in our household. We would put up a twelve-day Advent calendar, and at dinner each night, we'd light a candle and open another door. I rolled tablespoon-size balls of handmade fudge in sprinkles or nuts, wrapped them, and hung them on a wreath on the front door for the mailman and milkman. Christmas cards were strung on a ribbon and festooned the kitchen door.

On the Christmas Eve after Joe had moved out, I made sure the house looked as festive as in years past. I'd acquired a fresh-cut tree, and spent one afternoon with the children decorating it. We hung lights, silver tinsel, and glass ornaments purchased at Gertz or given to us by my brother, Larry, who worked for American Airlines and flew around the world. The crowning touch was angel hair—the silky white strands that enveloped the tree like a cloud. Our dog, Sheba, wandered around us as we decorated, sniffing at the presents. As usual, I had bought the children practical gifts—pajamas, slippers, bathrobes—but also something special for each, like a guitar for Michael and a paint set for Janet.

That afternoon, the doorbell rang. I ran to the door, expecting against hope that it would be Joe paying us a surprise visit. Or even better, to tell me he'd changed his mind and wanted to come back to his family.

Instead, a postal courier stood on the doorstep. "Mrs. Mrozowski?" he inquired.

"Yes?"

"Sign here." He handed me an envelope that had the return address of a lawyer.

After the postman left, I tore open the envelope to find papers informing me that Joe wanted a divorce. At first, I was annoyed. *He couldn't even wait until after Christmas?* Then I realized that my marriage was over. Joe was never coming back. I collapsed and rolled back and forth on the floor in my grief. It seemed as if the walls were tumbling around me.

Fortunately, the children weren't in the same room when this happened. I was able to keep myself together so that Christmas proceeded smoothly. The kids must have regretted that their father wasn't there, but at least they didn't know yet that he'd abandoned them. When I did tell them, Judith broke down crying and hugged Janet and Michael to her.

At least, I thought, I had my children. But not long after Joe left, Michael was taken away from me. He'd grown taller and stronger than me, and more mentally disturbed. One time he even swung at me with his fist, nearly knocking me to the ground. The agency didn't trust him without a man around the house. This broke my heart, but I recognized that I was unable to take care of Michael, and that keeping him in the house would make it unsafe for my daughters.

Judith was saddened by the loss of her little brother. Janet was relieved and more secure, although she also felt guilty for not missing him. Michael ended up being institutionalized at Kings Park Psychiatric Center on Long Island, where the girls and I were able to visit him a few times. Then, we were asked not to come anymore since our presence upset rather than helped him.

If there is any action that offered me a glimpse as to my cluelessness during this period of my life, it's my adoption of Michael. Michael had been intersex when he was born and had been surgically provided with a penis and assigned a masculine gender. He'd been in various foster homes before we took him into ours. Indeed, when we looked at Michael's records, we discovered that he'd been removed from his previous foster home because he'd tried to pour bleach down a three-year-old's throat. Yet, the agency had agreed to place him in a home with a child younger than him, Janet. We also found out that he was already writing and drawing violent pictures, which, in their manifestation of a deep socio-pathology, presaged his killing of the kittens, which in turn could have led to an outcome even worse for my daughters, especially Janet, than the attempted rape. Michael needed much more medical care and attention than our family could truly provide. For all the love and time we lavished on Michael, I now feel that it was reckless and negligent of me to have brought Michael into our home and to expose my daughters, especially Janet, to his rage and violence.

I was now confronted by complete failure. I had failed to create a safe space for my daughters in their home. I had failed to help Michael conquer his demons. I had failed to honor the vow I'd before God and the Catholic Church to keep my marriage intact. I had failed to keep my husband from having affairs with other women. I had failed to provide a more stable environment for my children than the one I had received from my own parents. And, for all my attempts to give my children the best, I'd failed to succeed in sustaining the kind of ordinary middle-class life that lay at the heart of the American dream.

In such circumstances, you always second-guess yourself. Could I have been more loving—less pragmatic, less concerned for us to get ahead? Had I mistaken love for Joe in the first place for a partnership based on striving to achieve material success rather than deepening our emotional lives and our spiritual practice, which Joe was so dismissive of? Joe was, in some way, looking for his mother in me. But was I, in some unconscious way, looking to be as dramatically self-sabotaging as my own mother? Had I too, entered into this marriage in as thoughtless a way as my own mother had with hers—with lust and immaturity covering up our inherent incompatibilities? Had I, in choosing a man who also had a volatile temper beneath his passivity, really wanted to replicate my mother's relationship with my father?

And then there was Michael. Had my rush to adopt him been not about him but an effort to bind my husband to our marriage, both of which relationships had dissolved with the departure of my son *and* husband within a few months of each other? Michael had been discarded by his father and by the remainder of his family. Had my pursuit of what I took to be godliness and charity in giving Michael a home and a family not in fact been a pious ego-trip—an expression of a shallow sanctimonious faith that was magical thinking? Did I think I had enough love within me to cover up all the cracks in my family life—enough love that would allow me to look the other way at the damaging and potentially life-threatening activities in my own home?

It's another source of great regret that I wasn't more aware through this time of how traumatized Janet had been by my failure to respond appropriately to Michael's illness. Janet seemed so self-contained—always climbing trees and reading a book amid their boughs—that I think I took her emotional strength for granted. She was such a dear child to me, and she needed me most because she was the youngest. She was quite accident-prone when she was growing up, and I fear that it's because I didn't give her the attention and affection that she needed.

After Michael and Joe left our household, I found myself asking myself over and over again: *What on earth have I done?* Gone were my dreams of the perfect family, the perfect marriage. I couldn't entertain the fact that my entire marriage had been a lie. I could barely wrap my head around the possibility of divorce. Sometimes, I wondered how I'd arrived in this situation. I'd tried to marry a man who wasn't like my father, who wasn't an abusive alcoholic. But instead, in trying to choose the opposite, I'd lived with a man who was passive aggressive. Maybe Joe was as wrong for me as my mother had been for my father.

Everything was falling to pieces around me, including my house. When Joe left, he hadn't finished renovating the basement and there was a big hole in the ground. I liked to think that he left it there so that one day, when I went downstairs, I would fall into it and break my neck. I had to spend money I didn't have to get a contractor in to complete the job. It was a good thing I did, though, because soon I'd be spending the better part of my days in that basement.

* * *

As it turned out, the end of our marriage was not as catastrophic as at first blush it threatened to be. It forced me to confront a reality—not merely in matters of my personal life, but in my spiritual practice as well. Over the years, I became reconciled to the fact that the divorce was good for Joe too. He'd suffered from an ulcer during our marriage, and after the divorce, it healed. Although Joe married Louise, I considered myself his wife until his death in 1988. After he passed away, I felt liberated, just as I imagine my mother had in the few years that remained to her after my father's death.

But at the time, the divorce led to the collapse of everything—my family, my social life, my world, my religion. Something had been missing in my spiritual life before then. I could resonate with the sacraments but I did so without any enthusiasm or joy. I seemed to have reached a plateau and was not nurtured by the rituals and rounds of the Catholic year, even though they are supposed to nurture and feed us. Once the divorce happened, the plateau became a downward slope.

Nor were illness and death finished with me. Not long after our parents passed away, my sister, Fran, was diagnosed with throat cancer. I helped her and her family through her treatments, and she recovered. Then, in 1971, Helen Porretta, my dear friend since childhood, who was like another sister to me, was diagnosed with breast cancer. During the four months she was sick, I accompanied her to every doctor's appointment and visited her every day. I watched how helpless she became as both the disease and the drugs that were supposed to save her, sapped the strength from her body. She'd wasted away to eighty pounds when she died, on Holy Friday. Helen left behind four children between the ages of five and nineteen, one of them Judith's childhood friend, Antoinette. I didn't understand why God could be so heartless.

I was thirty-nine years old when my marriage ended. During this time, I searched vainly for God and decided that not only did I have nothing to say to Him, but that I didn't believe He was even there. I concluded I must have created this God I'd been worshipping all these years. God must have been a figment of my imagination because I was doing everything that I was supposed to do and nothing had worked. This was like a death for me.

If this seems to you to be an immature response to the demands of faith, then you'd be correct. But then my faith was still, in essence, the faith of the child who'd accompanied her grandmother to church. It was deeply entwined with that little girl who'd wanted to escape into a world where she was loved unconditionally and whose virtue and piety were not only *seen* by God, but appreciated by Him. As a consequence, that faith was drenched in self-pity and saturated with self-righteous anger. How dare God not bless me with a fruitful marriage! How dare He let my friends and family members die on me! How dare God allow me to suffer when Joe was having the affairs and I'd expressed nothing but devotion and had played by the rules!

And when God refused to justify Himself to me, I decided not to justify myself to Him. This was not a sudden collapse, but a slow ebbing away of my faith, until all that was left was an empty stretch of sand. As I dropped Judith and Janet off at church, I would tell them I wouldn't be joining them because I didn't feel like it or I was too busy. Attending church scarcely seemed relevant amid the troubles in my marriage or the survival mode in which I found myself all too often. It was to get no easier.

Part II Welcome

4 Transformation

"Mom? Are you down there again?"

I looked up from my ironing board in the dim light of the basement. Judith and Janet were home from school. "Yes, I'm fine," I responded, answering the question Judith didn't dare ask.

"Okay," Judith said after a moment, and I heard her move away from the top of the stairs.

My girls were worried about me, but I didn't know how to reassure them that things were going to be all right. To be honest, I didn't know what would happen to us.

The years after Joe left me were some of the hardest in my life. As a single mother, I struggled with money because Joe didn't provide much child support or alimony. His reported income didn't include his under-the-table bonuses and commissions. The judge had to reach decisions based on the federally reported numbers, and since I had no way to substantiate the claims, Joe got away with paying far less than he should have. The child support payments he made arrived late, and when I asked him for extra money for Judith and Janet, he'd say no. Even though we were divorced, Joe and I were still arguing about money.

I constantly worried about bankruptcy and eviction. There were times when I thought I would have to go on welfare. I had no one to turn to. My relatives offered me no assistance. Thankfully, my great friends, the Silveris and the Dalools, were always available for me emotionally. However, the neighbors who used to invite Joe and me over for drinks stopped calling me. It was as if I were wearing the scarlet letter D for 'Divorcée.' At that time, the Catholic Church excommunicated divorcées and treated us as if we were to be shamed, or so I thought. I was also too proud to ask for help and didn't want anyone to suspect I was alone and struggling.

I worked from home, convincing myself that I needed to be there when my children returned from school. Judith and Janet were thirteen and ten years old respectively— tough years for any child, even with a father around. Since I had to be both parents, I became the disciplinarian, breadwinner, and homemaker. I was afraid the girls would suffer the consequences of a broken home. They needed the stability of a close-knit family and a calm household, and I would be their rock.

This is what I told myself. The truth was somewhat uglier. I was scared and angry, and I retreated from life. These emotions manifested themselves in a withdrawal of emotional engagement with my children. I put my tenderness aside and piled on the pounds by buffering myself with food. My kids worried about me. "What will we do if you die?" they asked me, obese and unhappy. "Don't worry," I replied. "My brother will look after you." As it turned out, the brother I meant was unstable, and it wouldn't have been at all appropriate for my children to be with him. Yet, I wasn't thinking clearly. I was a martinet: the girls had to act in a certain way, dress appropriately, place the cutlery on the table in the correct positions—as if the outward forms of discipline and 'proper' behavior would somehow compensate for my disordered and unbalanced inner world. Everything had to be perfect or you'd know exactly what infraction you'd committed, and at length. I was judgmental and inquisitorial. Unlike my mother with my siblings and me, I wanted to know exactly what Judith and Janet had been up to at school, but very like my mother, I easily resorted to criticism and comments.

I was under a great deal of stress. To earn money, I put an advertisement in the local penny-saver for home ironing. This was the time before drip-dry, when you just take the shirts out of the machine and place them on hangers, so ironing was essential. Soon I was ironing for what seemed like half of Plainview. I ironed eighteen hours a day, everything from sheets and pillowcases, to dresses and jeans. The bursitis in my shoulders became so painful that I required injections every few months. I earned five dollars an hour.

Instead of ironing upstairs in a light and airy room, I buried myself in the basement to do it, which, now I think of it, reflected where I was emotionally. The basement was divided into four small rooms. As you descended the steep stairs, Joe's workshop lay to the right. His tools were ordered on shelves, with nails, screws, nuts, and bolts sorted into small jars. He'd spend hours making wooden objects, including frames for his paint-by-number pictures. I also suspect that, like me, he disappeared into the basement to hide from his feelings.

Next to the workshop were the washer and dryer and the boiler room. Judith and Janet used to hide behind the boiler when they played hide-and-seek, and our dog, Sheba, gave birth to her litter of puppies on the warm dirt floor next to it. Joe had lined a third room with cedar so we could store our winter clothes there. I also used that room to keep my evening and cocktail dresses—all in a size two, which I could no longer wear. I figured that Judith snuck in and tried on those dresses because I'd discover them lying on the floor instead of hung up on the racks.

I set up my ironing board in the fourth room. It was cold and dark, like a cave, and I ironed in there as if I were mining for something. All those hours doing the same actions over and over offered me plenty of time to think. Memories from my childhood surfaced—the joy that had filled me in church, the fear that overcame me when my parents fought, and the sadness that washed over me when my grandmother died. Was that when I'd become so self-righteous? Was that when I started to judge my family and others around me, to keep myself from being harmed? I always believed I was correct about everything. I had opinions about what everyone said and did. I could hear myself and I didn't like it.

I wanted my false self to die. So I started to test God. "If you're there, show yourself to me because I don't believe in you." Sure enough, He never showed Himself— as if God were a kind of genie who could be summoned when I wanted him…

This continued for three years.

Judith helped me with my home business, sometimes ironing the shirts of her classmates' fathers. A few of her classmates were aware of what I did for a living, but it didn't keep Judith from being one of the most popular girls in school. In order to bring in some extra cash, I fostered some children for a couple hundred dollars a month. I enjoyed taking care of a pair of adorable twin boys named Glen and Daniel, who stayed with us for nine months while their single mother sorted her life out. Every foster child, though, was a painful reminder for me of Michael, the boy I'd lost, and I vowed not to repeat that mistake again.

So many things in our life were now absent. With the divorce, Joe kept the summer house in East Hampton (he promptly sold it), while I retained the home in Plainview. The neighbors' son, Paul Dalool, a friend and classmate of Judith's, helped out by mowing the lawn and trimming the hedges for me. To make ends meet, I rented out the second floor of the house as an apartment to a single girl and the bedroom on the first floor to a newlywed couple. We shared the bathroom with them and sometimes learned more about their private lives than we cared to. Once, when Judith and Janet were playing in the backyard, the breeze blew up the curtains and they glimpsed the couple having sex. The girls ran off laughing.

Judith, Janet, and I squeezed into the living room. We divided the space with louvered doors; one half was the sitting room with the TV, and the other our bedroom. All our beds were lined up in a row, including the bed for whatever foster child was staying with us at the time. It was difficult for anyone to get a good night's sleep (the children complained that I snored). Our situation resembled the crowded house on Shore Avenue when I was growing up, and how upset I'd been at having to share a room with my sister.

On Sunday, the day of rest and prayer, I insisted on a sit-down dinner with the girls. I would make a lavish, homemade meal of pasta with cake for dessert, and talk with them about their week. In the end, I reminded them, we were—and always would be—a family. The girls weren't allowed to complain on Sundays, though. 'Gripe Night,' as we called it, was reserved for Tuesday evening. "Don't talk to me right now," I would interrupt whenever they started to whine about something. "Wait until Gripe Night."

Although the girls had plenty to complain about, I realized they were keeping a lot of their hurt inside, especially regarding their mother. My critical attitude and judgmentalism continued, but I couldn't help it: I had so many pressures to keep them fed and clothed, a roof over our heads.

Occasionally, however, a softer side would come out in me.

Once, I caught Judith looking longingly at an advertisement in the local paper from B. Altman Department Store. It was an English tweed suit, Mary Quant-style, with a blue-and-red jacket and royal-blue skirt. It was perfect for a teenager in Beatlemania mode; Judith had once insisted on mutton for dinner because Paul McCartney had eaten it as a boy. I couldn't blame Judith for coveting the beautiful suit. I had brought her up to want the best of everything, if only because I hadn't had it as a child.

"Judith, you know that suit is too expensive," I told her.

"I know, Mother." She sighed and closed the paper.

My heart ached that I couldn't afford to buy my daughter one outfit she liked. "Do you really want that suit, Judith?"

"Yes."

"Then we'll get it."

And we did. It was a brief moment of indulgent pleasure in what was a very tough period of our lives.

The person I was harshest on was myself. For two years after Joe left, I thought about him every day. I thought more about him after we were no longer married than during the time we *were*. He was the total focus of my life. I constantly dwelled on my jealousy, hate, anger, and frustration, some of it, I admit, sexual. I was consumed with feeling like a victim. Of course, I did this with a lot of class! I didn't break dishes or unloose any four-letter words. But what emerged from my mouth—insidious and meant to hurt—was perhaps worse than any ordinary vulgarities.

When Joe arrived to pick up the girls on Saturdays, I wouldn't go to the door or even look at him because my blood pressure would soar. After they came home, I had a ritual. I would give them cookies and milk and then pump them for information.

"How was it being with your father?" I'd ask.

"We had a good time," they'd reply cautiously.

"Where'd you go for dinner?"

"Howard Johnson's."

"Oh, *that* place again."

I was venomous—as gossipy and catty as my mother had been.

Then one day, Judith reported that she'd been sitting in the front seat of the car with her father, and had pulled down the sun-visor to see a Polaroid photo of a blond woman. She'd asked Joe who the woman was, not knowing it was Louise. Joe and I had been careful to hide Louise's role in the divorce from our children.

"Dad said she is the woman he loves and they plan to get married," Judith announced.

Something in me snapped. "Isn't that wonderful?" I responded, my voice dripping with sarcasm. "Well, I guess he has the right to be happy. And don't worry, because God forgives adultery."

I can't forget the shocked look on Judith's face after those words spewed from my mouth. I'd built a wall around myself and become rigid and unyielding so that no one could hurt me. But I realized the opposite was happening— I was harming my children and myself with my hatred and anger.

That night when I retired to bed, I prayed I would die. *God, take me. This is destroying the children. I don't want to live another minute.* Fortunately, God was not that accommodating of my selfishness and self-righteousness. He wasn't going to allow me out of the situation quite so easily.

The next day, I went to buy some starch for ironing the shirts and ran across a bookstore with marked-down books, including *The Power of Positive Thinking* by Norman Vincent Peale. It cost only a quarter so I could afford it. This book, which had been first published the year Judith was born, had been popular for years. I'd never paid serious attention to it before, though.

Peale had reprinted a simple little prayer for reconciliation by his friend, H. C. Mattern:

"The way to happiness: Keep your heart free from hate, your mind from worry. Live simply, expect little, and give much. Fill your life with love. Scatter sunshine. Forget self, think of others. Do as you would be done by."

The wisdom of Mattern's prayer was straightforward and yet, challenging. I wasn't seeking reconciliation, but I was looking to be released from this terrible anger. I would recite the Our Father and sit in a chair while the girls went off to school. I did the work of visualizing and allowing Joe to come into this space, deep within my heart. In my imagination, face-to-face, I would tell him how he had hurt me, every little detail.

You put me down me whenever I talked to our children about God.

You refused to give me ownership over the money I earned.

You accused me of having affairs when you were the one who was having an affair behind my back.

You insisted on getting a divorce when I did everything I could to reconcile our differences and made every effort to please you.

You broke up our home for our precious girls.

You.

You.

You.

Then I would look at him and say, "I forgive you."

That was the foundation of the Forgiveness Prayer. (See Chapter 9.)

In the beginning, I found it next to impossible to forgive Joe. The words stuck in my throat, but I finally blurted them out. Then, as I was visualizing, I would ask Joe how he thought he'd hurt me. At first, he didn't say anything, which was natural, because of course, he wouldn't think he'd done anything wrong. *He* was perfect. But I continued to ask him anyway. I conducted this practice twice a day, seven days a week, for seven months. We'd been married for almost twenty years, so I had a lot to forgive!

Then one Sunday morning, the telephone rang. I picked up the receiver and was surprised to find Joe on the line. He didn't call me any more than he had to, and I can't say I blame him. I always employed a cutting tone and he never anticipated what I would say next.

"Is everything all right, Joe?" I asked.

He said it was, and then added, "How are you feeling?"

"Okay, I guess." I was so stunned to hear him ask about my well-being that I didn't know how to answer.

Gradually, Joe began to open up to me. He talked about Louise and her children, whom I'd only heard a little bit about before. Judith and Janet would tell me that when they visited their father, Louise would brag about her children to their faces. Or Louise would be sour and mean, or ignore them altogether. Now I learned that Louise's eldest, a daughter, lived in Marquette, Michigan, with her family; the first son was an inventor in Connecticut, and the second son was a college student and lived at home.

Joe and I spent about five minutes on the phone together, talking civilly to each other. Then the girls came to the phone to talk to their father.

Afterward, while we were eating breakfast, Judith said, "Gee, Mother, we were wondering who you were talking to. We were trying to guess, and I told Janet that you were talking to Dad. Janet said, 'No way, she'd never talk to Dad that way. That's not Dad on the phone.'"

But it was. A deep change had occurred in me. From then on, my relationship with Joe was different. He and I were able to communicate, to share in our children's milestones. Such a transformation was all due to that one simple practice of forgiveness, one that I would need to employ later when I attempted to forgive the other man in my life who'd failed me—my father.

The root of that ability to forgive grew from *The Power of Positive Thinking* by Norman Vincent Peale. That book taught me so much. I could empathize with Dr. Peale, a minster's son who had been weighed down by the pressure of following in his father's footsteps. He was afraid of public speaking and did not like his physical appearance as a young man because he was so skinny. In the book, Dr. Peale recommends emptying the mind twice a day and using suggestive articulation, which is not unlike centering prayer. Several of his other statements resonated with me.

There are various causes of inferiority feelings, and not a few stem from childhood... The greatest secret for eliminating the inferiority complex...is to fill your mind to overflowing with faith.

My childhood had been full of small injustices and resentments, so that I retreated from family life into a spiritual life.

Faith power works wonders.

I had prayed to God and St. Jude for a child and my daughters had come into my life.

Many of us manufacture our own unhappiness.

I had been busy, manufacturing for years, by being so angry at Joe.

On Sunday afternoons, I'd quote sections from the book to Judith and Janet, and the three of us would practice the power of positive thinking. We'd become conscious of our daily negative thoughts and would remind one another to replace them with positive ones. In this way, we were becoming self-directed therapists without even knowing it. At the end of our sessions, I would put Harry Belafonte records such as 'Day-o' on the gramophone and the three of us would dance around.

I was beginning to see the effects of Dr. Peale's practical spirituality on my psyche. Fortunately for us, Dr. Peale was a minister at Marble Collegiate Church in Manhattan, so one day, I took the girls into the city to hear him speak. I saw Judith and Janet look up at the church's arched ceiling with the same awed expressions I had as a child at St. Pius. Dr. Peale was a balding man in spectacles and a black robe. He looked small in his pulpit from far away, but his lively gestures and booming voice filled the cavernous church. Pounding the lectern, he read the verse from Philippians 4:6: "Have no anxiety about anything, but in everything by prayer and supplication with thanksgiving, let your requests be made known to God."

I started to think, if *The Power of Positive Thinking* helped me heal, what else could I read that might re-instill my faith in God? I became thirsty to gain more knowledge and decided to start from the very beginning.

I belonged to the library in the nearby town of Ronkonkoma, and for ten cents, I could take out as many books as I wanted. I would visit the library once a month, pay my ten cents, and return home with lots of spiritual books. Now that I had lost my belief in God, I wanted to know more about Him. I set up a book-holder by my ironing board, and as I performed the mundane, repetitive task of ironing, I flipped the pages and filled my mind.

I read a great deal of spiritual literature, including that by Thomas Merton, Joseph Campbell, Pierre Teilhard de Chardin, the Desert Fathers, St. Thomas Aquinas, St. John of the Cross, St. Teresa of Ávila, and St. Catherine of Siena. All of these practitioners and thinkers had one thing in common: they perceived the awesome power of the ineffable and how much we human beings rely on forces beyond our immediate controlling consciousness. In the confines of their cells or caves, or focused on the extraordinary mysteries of the cosmos, or reflecting on the common threads that tie the world's religious systems together, these men and women had confronted the human being not only at its most exalted, creative, and expressive, but also at its most vulnerable, needy, and dependent.

It became clear to me, through the course of several years of engaging with spiritual literature, that attending church or mouthing pieties or even raging and shaking my fist at God were merely the cheap vestments of faith. They had their place as responses to the divine, but they didn't get to the heart of what the German theologian, Rudolf Otto, called in *The Idea of the Holy,* the *mysterium tremendum et fascinans*: the mystery that is at once terrifying and fascinating. As the Letter to the Hebrews writes, "It is a dreadful thing to fall into the hands of the living God" (10:31), and I began to see that faith in God was not something you worked at or pushed your way toward, but something you opened yourself up to receive—with all the agony and self-exposure that might attend a heart cracked by desperation or flung upon the ground in agony.

For all of the sorrow I'd gone through, all of the losses, I had, in fact, not opened myself to God. In fact, like Jonah, I'd tried to avoid Him, or wall myself up from my emotions. What I needed is what Thomas Keating has called 'divine therapy': whereby God would come in and heal all the pathologies that my false self had developed, and continued to develop, to protect me from genuine healing and, perversely, keep me away from that which I truly desired, which was intimacy with God. What I didn't realize then, as the tiny, hairline cracks in my heart began to open as I read these books, was that the process would take the rest of my life.

As it stood in the mid-1960s, I still retained major doubts and I was painfully literal in my interpretations. When I read about St. Catherine of Siena's 'mystical marriage' to God, I questioned the source of her faith. In my life, I had tried to do everything right, yet my marriage had fallen apart.

Then I thought, *What St. Catherine of Siena did, I can do.*

I decided that instead of running into the arms of another man, I would attempt to fall into the arms of God. Perhaps God would let me live my life in Him and through Him. Perhaps He would let me share with Him the fullness of life and dispel the obstacles that made me think that I was separated from Him and from others.

The first thing I needed to do was to continue reading and thinking, and to do a lot more forgiving—not only of

Joe, but everyone I'd come across. I had to work on releasing my controlling ego, my judgmental nature, my constant desire to be right. I needed to practice loving kindness and detachment, which was the path of true awakening. This would require more humility and openness than I might be able yet to master. But, at least I was on my way.

5 Prayer

One evening, not long after the end of my marriage became official, I was pacing back and forth across the floor of my living room, full of doubt. I couldn't decide whether I should attend a lecture being held by the Sisters of the Cenacle in Ronkonkoma. I was very familiar with the Cenacle, as I'd attended spiritual retreats and taught religious education to children there. One of the nuns, Sr. Thelma Hall, was my spiritual director, offering me guidance on how to rediscover and deepen my relationship with God.

That night, a priest from the Tribunal was scheduled to give a talk to separated and divorced Catholics. I wanted to hear what he had to say, but I was also worried about other people finding out I was divorced. In 1968, separated and divorced Catholics were still considered anathema and not allowed to take Communion.

I said to Judith and Janet, "I think I'm going to the Cenacle to hear a lecture tonight. It costs three dollars to get in."

"That's great, Mother," Judith responded, seeming genuinely happy.

Then I reconsidered, "Actually, I'm not sure if I should go."

My daughters exchanged looks. "If it's the three dollars," Janet suggested, "we'll give it to you, Mom."

With such supportive daughters, how could I not go?

When I arrived at the Cenacle, the venue was packed. One-hundred and fifty people attended this lecture and two-hundred people were turned away. Obviously there were many separated and divorced Catholics who felt like I did. When I became a divorcée, I reckoned I didn't have a problem—the Church did, and I wasn't about to leave! We were all 'coming out of the closet,' so to speak. The priest spoke about the spiritual and emotional necessities of separated and divorced Catholics, how we needed ministry as much as everyone else. This sparked something inside me, but I didn't do anything about it for the next two years, until after Judith had departed for college.

As someone who hadn't been allowed to finish high school, I always made my children's education a priority. Judith cared about her schoolwork and studies, but had a more difficult time staying focused because she was distressed by the breakdown of the family. During this time, she depended on school and her friends as a support system to keep her sane.

I looked long and hard into the question of where Judith should go to college. My old friend, Helen Martin, had a relative who'd gone to St. Mary-of-the-Woods in Terre Haute, Indiana. It seemed like a safe place, far from all the drug use, free love, and political protests occurring at the time. Every parent was afraid their child would either be called up, or become involved in the anti-Vietnam War movement and be killed. In fact, one of Judith's classmates from Plainview High School had been a victim of the shootings at Kent State in 1970. What better place to go to college than an all-girls' school in the Midwest? Besides, Judith's childhood friend, Antoinette Porretta, daughter of my best friend, Helen, also was attending St. Mary's, and the girls didn't want to be separated.

Judith was accepted to college. I was relieved, but also worried. How would I afford the tuition? I decided to fix up our house and sell it. With the help of my brother, Peter, and brother-in-law, Al, I refinished the bathroom and found a buyer. The summer before Judith departed for school, we moved fifteen miles southeast, from Plainview to North Babylon. Our new home was a rental in the Somerset Village Apartments on August Road.

Enough money was left over from the sale for us to purchase some new furniture. I bought a round table with curved director chairs that swiveled for the kitchen. For the dining room, I acquired a colonial-style set from Ethan Allen, complete with hutch, table, and four ladder-back chairs made out of dark espresso-stained pine. The walnut-stained pine living room furniture also came from Ethan Allen. I made floor-to-ceiling, ruffled curtains for that room, and bought pale blue tapestry curtains for my bedroom to match the bedcover. The furniture in that room was the maple bedroom set I'd owned since I was married. The girls' room contained a set with beds, dressers, desk, and bookshelf made out of white Formica. I was also able to obtain the car of my dreams, a maroon Cadillac Eldorado with a black leather interior. After years of old furniture and a beat-up station wagon—all of which reminded me of my failed marriage—I was ready for a new start, and so were the girls.

In elementary school, Janet encountered troubles with the fourth-grade teacher, who was biased and paid attention to a small group of kids, neglecting her and others in the class. Janet, who was a bright and intelligent student, almost failed to pass her grade, a situation I put down to the problems she was experiencing at home, as well as the lack of support of school. I decided she needed more stability, so I placed her at the Academy of St. Joseph in Brentwood, on a need-based partial scholarship. When Judith left for college, Janet suspected she might be missing something by being educated at an all-girls' school and started to attend Plainview High School, where Judith had been a student. After three months, however, Janet found public high school unbearable. The classes were too large and the boys were distracting. She also had a biology teacher who treated her badly, saving the most difficult questions for Janet and addressing her by nicknames based on her appearance. Janet, who was a radiant young woman, with long blond hair, large blue eyes, and a slim, athletic figure, was always dressed neatly and modestly, which you wouldn't think would pose a problem for the school. However, as Janet reported to me one day, the teacher had called her 'Miss Priss.'

At one point in my life, I would have been enraged on Janet's behalf. Now, I knew better and remained calm. "Janet," I advised, "you need to be respectful to the teacher and not succumb to any desire to return any anger and nastiness you may receive."

Janet sniffled and nodded, "Mom, can I please go back to St. Joseph's?"

"We'll see," I replied. "For now, you need to combat your teacher's unfairness and cruelty with goodness from your heart."

From that day on, Janet over-prepared for every class. When the teacher asked her a difficult question, she'd respond, "Thank you for calling on me," and give the correct answer. The first time Janet tried this tactic, she arrived home beaming. The teacher had been completely caught off-guard. As it turned out, the teacher grew to like and respect Janet, and started calling her by her real name. Three months later, when Janet departed Plainview High School to return to the Academy of St. Joseph—this time on an academic-based scholarship—the teacher cried and confessed to Janet that she would miss her. I think Janet's approach had truly touched and transformed this woman. At least, she'd never tease a student again!

It's my belief that this episode offered a good lesson for Janet—and for me. My younger daughter learned that although she couldn't control someone else's treatment of, or response to, her, she could most certainly control her own. She could choose to rise to the occasion and not lower herself to a behavior that was both foreign to her and beneath her standards. Although I thought of this as 'killing with kindness,' it was really a nonviolent approach toward dealing with the difficulties in life, and was, in its own way, a response to our reading of Norman Vincent Peale. I also learned the value of patience and forbearance in not allowing any overheated or histrionic response I may have had to Janet's telling me about her teacher—*How dare she!*

Wait until I give her a piece of my mind! Instead, I saw how valuable it is to mirror the kind of behavior you want in your child, and honor *their* feelings rather than impose your own. Janet didn't want me to make it harder for her; she wanted me to help her. On *this* occasion, at least, I like to think, I responded to Janet's needs appropriately and effectively.

When Janet had been attending middle school at St. Joseph's, she'd had a classmate named Jeanette. I became friends with Jeanette's mother, who introduced me to her friend, Barbara, a medical administrator at Brunswick Hospital Center in Amityville. I was still doing a little home ironing on the side, but in my spare time, I'd studied to become a medical secretary and was working for a doctor in town. I'd also earned my G.E.D. (General Educational Development) certificate, an exciting and proud moment for me. More than twenty years after I'd been forced to leave high school, I finally acquired a diploma.

After I moved to North Babylon, Barbara informed me of a job opening for an administrative assistant at Brunswick, which was a mental hospital. I ended up working with her in the worst ward, Carlin Hall, which was filled with violent women and the most extreme cases. Barbara and I referred to ourselves as 'Snoopy and Woodstock,' from Charles M. Schulz's Peanuts comic strip, with me being Woodstock—the wise and efficient (if occasionally exasperated) bird who looks out for Snoopy. I encouraged Barbara to work for a doctorate so she could apply to become the head of the Brunswick nursing staff. While she was busy furthering her education, I helped develop and expand many of the programs, such as those for alcoholics, that she received credit for. I was the solid ground she walked upon.

I often had to work double shifts because I was still experiencing financial difficulties. But I could count on Janet to help me out at home. She cleaned the house, washed and ironed the clothes, and walked into town for groceries. She never complained that she had to perform these chores, or that she received angry telephone calls from creditors. Sometimes, when she returned home after school, the power would be out because I couldn't pay the electricity bill.

When I wasn't working nights at the hospital, I'd visit prayer groups at the church of Sts. Cyril and Methodius in Deer Park, and the Good Samaritan Hospital in West Islip. I also continued to see Sr. Thelma Hall from the Cenacle for spiritual guidance. By this time, Sr. Thelma had started a small group of separated and divorced Catholics that I also joined. With the backing of Fr. Fred Schaefer of St. Brigid's Parish in Westbury, we decided to expand the group on Long Island and put an ad in the local papers.

At that first meeting, I stood at the front door of the church, as always dressed in high heels, my long fingernails painted red, and my hair in a French roll. As each person passed by, I handed them a Good News Bible. All too soon, I ran out of copies. We'd expected thirty people to show up, but as on that evening of the talk at the Cenacle, hundreds arrived to demonstrate that even though they were separated and divorced, they still wanted to be part of the Church. That's how the Long Island Chapter of Separated and Divorced Catholics was born.

Divorce, as I would describe in the meetings I led, was a kind of dying, in which we pass through the five stages of grief (denial, anger, bargaining, depression, and acceptance) much as the Swiss psychiatrist, Elisabeth Kübler-Ross, lists in her seminal work, *On Death and Dying*. I indicated that in the traumatic aftermath of divorce, an individual might behave quite irrationally—keeping excessively busy, taking pills, drinking, and engaging in promiscuous behavior. I then talked about how our marriages had often been to people wholly unlike ourselves, and that we'd spent a huge amount of our married life trying to change them. Why did we feel the need to do this? And why were we constantly attempting to make them feel good or happy? Was it a way to compensate for our own low opinion of ourselves or our own unhappiness? If so, I suggested, we needed to ask ourselves another question: "What am I lacking in myself that I need this constant approval?"

I concluded the meetings by suggesting that we were obligated to pay attention to our lives, and that before we entered into a relationship, we needed to become aware of our own uniqueness and have a deep appreciation for ourselves and who we were. This entailed developing enough self-esteem that we wouldn't simply surrender our love, respect, and appreciation unless we owned these ourselves.

Obviously, in sharing my ideas, I was drawing deeply on my own relationship with Joe and my reactions to, and behaviors following, our divorce. I found this articulation and solidarity with others deeply healing. Although the chapter held a number of secular activities, such as parties and dances, it was important to me to introduce a spiritual element. I organized retreats and held a Bible Study group once a week on Tuesday nights, which I facilitated because I was still searching for God. I called the program G.I.F.T.S., which stood for 'Groups in Faith to Share.' Before we started the study group meeting, we'd keep fifteen minutes of silence. At the time, I didn't know that engaging in this silence was a form of centering prayer. I simply thought we'd have some time to quiet people down as they arrived and before we began talking about the Bible. It was a non-conceptual time, with no images and no worries—just people transitioning from their busy world and sitting quietly before beginning to read scripture.

When I disclosed to Sr. Thelma about our reading at Bible Study, she exclaimed, "That's *lectio divina*!"

"What's that?" I asked. I was totally ignorant of this spiritual practice.

Sr. Thelma, who would later write a book on the practice called *Too Deep for Words*, explained to me how *lectio divina*, which is Latin for 'divine reading,' was an organic process of prayer taught for the first 1,600 years of the Church. She informed me that it was how Christians entered spiritual formation, through listening or reading the divine word. This was because in the very early Church, most people didn't read, so they listened to the word of God either at the liturgies, or when small communities gathered to pray. They heard stories about Jesus Christ, and after three-hundred years, this process of prayer was established.

I also learned that *lectio divina* is like having a one-on-one discussion with God—or, as Thomas Keating says in *Open Mind, Open Heart*, "a way of listening to the texts of scripture as if we were in conversation with Christ." The first movement of the practice is *lectio*, or reading, which we listen to with our hearts. The second is *meditatio*, or meditation, where we use our minds to reflect upon the word. The third is *oratio*, or prayer, which is when we express the effect the words have on us as a person. The fourth movement is called *contemplatio*, or resting in God, where we let God do the work. By engaging in *lectio divina*, we're not being exegetes. The aim is not to parse or understand the theological meaning of a passage. We're not practicing what biblical scholars call 'form criticism,' which means analyzing a passage to determine which segments may be original and which may be later additions to the text, to discern the passage's original intent. We're also not looking for moral instruction or prescriptions for the spiritual life. *Lectio divina* is, or aims to be, a much deeper, much more internal way of responding to scripture. Through it, we're developing a relationship with God— forming an acquaintanceship, finding out more about the other person, and interacting in a manner that, through the word, becomes deeper than words. As I liked to tell people with a certain facetiousness, *lectio divina* was like going on heavy dates with Jesus.

Over time, I could see the effect of *lectio divina* on the people in Bible Study. Like me, these people had been totally torn apart. They'd put their faith on a shelf because they weren't sure they believed anymore, not only in God and the Church, but in themselves. What all of us who practiced *lectio divina* hoped was that the sacred word would begin to settle in us and start to heal us, acting as the divine therapist, by bringing us closer to God.

This was certainly my experience. Yet, as I began to open up, dangers lurked. After Bible Study, people would come to me and say things like, "Mary, that study was so wonderful. You have such great insights. Thank you." The fires of my vanity and need for approval, which continued to smolder inside me, were stoked. I started walking around like the Messiah. I uttered things like, "We know it's God doing the work. Isn't God wonderful? Look what he does for us!" On the deepest level of my being, I felt an incredible satisfaction, without realizing what all this self-satisfaction was doing to me.

A few years into Bible Study, we started holding our meetings in the evenings at a local school. I was given the keys to the classroom, which was like being handed the keys to the kingdom. One beautiful fall night, with a full moon lighting up the sky, I locked up after the meeting. It was like locking up Heaven. I stood in the parking lot, staring up at the moon and filled with wonderment, when all of a sudden, I heard a voice deep inside me.

It's not for the others that you're here, it's for you because you need it.

It was as if God were speaking to me through a megaphone.

I was crushed. I was fixed to the spot, thinking about my motivations. All this time, I'd been so full of myself, believing I was performing a great service by helping everyone in the group, when I was really the one who needed help. Chastened, I returned to Bible Study the following Tuesday, but my perception and facilitation of the meeting were different. My whole attitude had changed because, in the parking lot under the full moon, I'd been exposed to my intentions. I thought the whole world had been witness to it, but the conversation had taken place only between myself and God.

I perceived that eventually I would have to give up the Bible Study, for the good of my spiritual development and for the people in the group. Not only were they becoming overly dependent on me, but I was becoming too satisfied by their dependence, too concerned that I would be indispensable. The prayer group had, in essence, become another way to establish the false self's program for happiness—in particular, my wish to control and to be wanted. To be clear, it wasn't that I hadn't accomplished something genuine and useful for people; I'd made many good friends there, and these friendships would last for many years to come. But the call to a deeper relationship with God sometimes means giving up what is comfortable and affirming in our religious practice (the adult equivalent of my childhood enjoyment of attending church) for something more intimate, scary, and perhaps even more soul-scouring: the terrible, wonderful arms of God.

As it turns out, I continued to hold prayer groups and workshops in later years, but that Bible Study group was the first and longest of them all. It not only introduced me to contemplative practices, but showed me how much I still had to learn on my spiritual path.

6 Practice

The church was alive with light and music.

"Our inheritance is to be present to the Trinity, to the Father, the Son, and the Spirit that dwells within us," the priest intoned. "I think if you remember at Pentecost, Jesus said, 'I've come. I'm going to leave you physically, but I will not leave you alone. I will send the comforter, the paraclete, the Holy Spirit.' That's your birthday gift and my birthday gift, because Pentecost is the birthday of the Church."

I looked at the other people around me. We all lifted our hands toward the sky and opened our mouths in song,

"Spirit of the living God, fall afresh on me
Spirit of the living God, fall afresh on me
Melt me, mold me, fill me, use me
Spirit of the living God, fall afresh on me.
Spirit of the living God, move among us all
Make us one in heart and mind, make us one in love
Humble, caring, selfless, sharing
Spirit of the living God, fill our lives with love."

I'd been involved with the Charismatic Renewal on Long Island since 1972. The movement had been initiated in 1967, in the wake of the Second Vatican Council and centered on the idea of a renewed Pentecost, a fresh baptism of the Holy Spirit, which was different from the Protestant Pentecostal tradition by grounding itself within the rituals and order of the Roman Catholic Church. What was new, and in the spirit of Vatican II, was that everyone, not just the ordained, was able to receive the *charisms*, or gifts, of the Holy Spirit.

Although I'd been attending the Cenacle and engaged with prayer groups for years, the Renewal was unlike anything I'd ever encountered before. I was on fire with the love of God. Even though I didn't have a strong voice, I loved to sing. I made more friends than I'd ever had before, and people asked me for advice and companionship. I looked forward to waking up and seeing what the day had in store for me. It was like I'd fallen in love with life again, and I dearly wanted Judith and Janet to share in my journey.

Social work seemed to be Judith's calling. She started the first drug hotline at Indiana State University, volunteered at an all-boys orphanage on weekends, and was a member of the first class to graduate from her school's department in social work. After college, she returned home to undertake graduate studies in that field at Fordham University.

At the time, Janet was also living at home. She'd received a scholarship to the State University of New York at Buffalo, and wanted to study pre-medicine, but after the first year, had suffered for six months of strep throat and swollen glands. She returned home in the spring of her sophomore year for surgery on her tonsils, and never returned to Buffalo. Instead, she entered a program at the

Katharine Gibbs School in the city to become an executive secretary.

I enjoyed having both my daughters living with me again, but we couldn't afford the apartment in North Babylon anymore. We returned to Plainview where the ever-compassionate, Angelo and Connie Silveri, offered us the use of the apartment, at a very reasonable rent, on the second floor of their house. The place was small, but we managed. I even invited Patty, a friend of Judith's from college, who'd been offered a job as a buyer at Gimbels' department store, to stay with us for a while. I decorated the living room beautifully with a white rug, a zebra-striped couch, and a print of the Georgia O'Keefe painting, 'The White Calico Flower.'

Whenever my daughters were home, I constantly praised the Renewal, blasted the music, and scattered the literature around. I'm sure I was insufferable, and looking back on myself twenty years on, I can see that the kind of religious mania I was undergoing was, in its own way, no different from the 'uppers' I still took to help me deal with my weight problem. God, in such circumstances, was another drug to make me feel good about myself. It wasn't necessarily feeding my ego in the same way that *lectio divina* was in danger of doing, and, goodness knows, I was more affirming of life than I had been in a long time, but I was nonetheless hopped up on a diet of the kind of emotional excess that often accompanies the newly converted. My children enjoyed attending the Renewal gatherings; I think they found it fun. But they were young women now, and they'd seen enough of my highs and lows throughout the years to be skeptical about my newfound enthusiasm.

Nonetheless, I persevered. In May of 1975, I decided to take Judith and Janet with me to the Ninth International Congress for Charismatic Catholics in Rome, Italy. I was convinced that after a few days, they'd be singing louder than anyone else if I could steal them away for a while. I lured them in by calling the trip a 'Roman Holiday.' Afterward, we'd visit Florence and then Munich, Germany, via sleeper-train.

We stayed in the town of Frascati, just outside of Rome, and traveled into the city every day for the conference, which was held over the catacombs. It was the first international trip for all of us, and it was eye-opening for the girls in more ways than one. Once, when we were on the bus from the hotel to the conference, a man pinched Judith's butt and she screamed out loud! After we recovered from our shock, we found it hilarious.

I'd wanted the girls to discover God in the Eternal City, but instead, I was the one who received enlightenment. More than ten-thousand attended the conference, and I met many remarkable people who were on a similar journey to mine. On the last day, during Mass at St. Peter's Basilica, we listened to Pope Paul VI say, "For all of us, this renewal and reconciliation is a further development of the grace of divine adoption, the grace of our sacramental Baptism into Christ Jesus and into his death, in order that we might walk in the newness of life." The Congress was also where I first heard the question, "What is centering prayer?" and felt the call to answer it.

Truth be told, centering prayer had never wholly died within the Christian tradition, but had gone into abeyance. In 1971, Pope Paul VI had asked the superior generals of all the abbeys and monasteries (who included Thomas Keating, then abbot of St. Joseph's Abbey in Spencer, Massachusetts) to extrapolate the contemplative dimension of the Gospel from the Christian tradition for the benefit of monastics and laypeople. The contemplative dimension had been part of the Christian tradition from the earliest periods in Church history, from the time of Anthony the Great (251-356), John Cassian (360-435), and Gregory the Great (540-604). But, apart from the practice of a very few saints, whose work I mentioned in an earlier chapter, the Church had oriented most Christians toward the more doctrinal or apostolic forms of Christian life. In other words, the Church had, in recent centuries, emphasized the outward aspects of religious practice—conforming to the manifestations of spiritual life and good works—rather than the interior, contemplative, or mystical.

Since Swami Vivekananda's presence at the first Parliament of the World's Religions in Chicago in 1983, South and East Asian religious practices had been making inroads in the West, while other means of transforming one's consciousness (such as marijuana and LSD) were opening people up to alternative psycho-mystical occurrences. The Beat poets, the writer, Christopher Isherwood, and the Beatles had put non-Western religions firmly in the public sphere by the late 1960s. Thomas Merton had engaged in dialogue and corresponded with His Holiness, the Dalai Lama, and with D. T. Suzuki, the great scholar of Zen Buddhism. As a result, many earnest spiritual seekers and young people were traveling to East and South Asia to learn non-conceptual meditation techniques. Pope Paul VI concluded that Christianity was missing a huge opportunity to provide those looking for a deeper relationship with the divine, and who were leaving the Church because they judged it too doctrinal and externally focused, with a means of discovering what their own tradition offered. He wanted to renew the contemplative tradition in the Christian churches, because it was very much part of the Christian faith.

Three monks in the Trappist order—Frs. Thomas Keating, William Meninger, and Basil Pennington—took the fourteenth-century classic, *The Cloud of Unknowing,* and the history of St. Anthony by Athanasius of Alexandria, and put together a method called 'The Prayer of *The Cloud*,' which would be taught to those on retreat at St. Joseph's Abbey, where the three monks resided. It was determined that the prayer couldn't be learned from books or study, but would need to be practiced, methodically. Retreatants would pray using the technique at least twice a day, for twenty minutes each time. It was understood that the prayer wouldn't be a substitute for other forms of prayer, but should be conceived as a method of nonverbal prayer—contemplation along the same lines as *lectio divina*. Indeed, *lectio* would form a basis for the development of centering prayer.

Shortly thereafter, it was noticed that Thomas Merton had described contemplative prayer as 'centered entirely on the presence of God,' and the name of the prayer was changed to 'centering prayer.' Sr. Thelma Hall had attended the first centering prayer retreat that Fr. Keating held in

Spencer, in 1977. (In 1981, he retired as abbot and moved to St. Benedict's Monastery in Snowmass, Colorado.)

Centering prayer is a receptive, non-conceptual prayer that goes beyond words. It calls us simply to rest and remain in the presence of God as a way of exercising our faith. As the words 'call' and 'exercise' suggest, this process is a matter of vocation, as well as evocation, of discipline and practice, as well as allowing the presence of God to come upon you. As such, centering prayer fosters humility, intimacy, and a going within, in order to allow the spirit of God to remove the obstacles that have kept us apart from Him. These obstacles may appear to take the form of darkness or shadows, or the tendencies or tics within us that we don't like and which we want to hide from ourselves and not deal with. (God knows, I had enough of them!)

The essence, even genius, of centering prayer lies in what it is not. It doesn't consist of pleas for forgiveness or redemption; we're not in a confessional or kneeling before an altar. Our goal is not to be more charitable, or more pious, or more doctrinally sound—although, through the practice of centering prayer, these fruits and gifts of the spirit may manifest themselves as such. Nor are we attempting to justify our behavior, make claims on God on behalf of our virtue, or bargain for a better outcome for ourselves or our loved ones. If nothing else, centering prayer makes very clear how far we are away from being in a position to ask those things of God! The heart of centering prayer is its receptivity to God. For who knows us more closely, more honestly, more lovingly, and more compassionately than God? The more we open up that interior space to God, the more God pours his love into us, which in turn allows those obstacles—those seemingly impenetrable barriers, insurmountable walls, and unbridgeable chasms—to dissolve.

When I first heard about centering prayer, I was immediately attracted to the idea of an intimate, personal relationship with God. I didn't quite understand the process, though. Indeed, it all seemed very mysterious, even arcane, to me, which isn't surprising, because centering prayer is what is known as an apophatic form of prayer, which means the way of not-knowing, or the *via negativa*. It expresses its interiority by taking the cue from Jesus' words in Matthew 6:6: "But when you pray, go into your room and shut the door and pray to your Father who is in secret; and your Father who sees in secret will reward you." The inner room is a conceptual space that emphasizes the intimacy of God, and the need for quiet and the tuning-out of the distractions of the outside world. This space is a safe zone where the false self and its programs for happiness can be purged—including all those preconceptions we have about our faith. For, as Thomas Keating writes in *Invitation to Love*: "Our preconceived ideas and prepackaged value system are obstacles to grace."

Therefore, centering prayer aims to rid the mind of notions about God, Jesus, the Holy Spirit, faith, self, and all of the constructs that we erect as a means of organizing our consciousness toward a goal. It's about stripping away some of those concepts about God that we may have used to buttress an immature or complacent self, to reveal a more authentic and richer relationship with the divine. Within the space we provide for centering prayer—those twenty minutes, twice a day—we attempt to surrender everything to God and trust in Him.

All that I have written above may sound overly conceptual, even intimidating. But one way to understand it is through a story I often tell. (The story comes in many different versions, and has many sources, so I'm not claiming any originality here.)

There was once a popular professor, who had many students and was well-known for his wisdom. After class one day, he returned home, only to find, when he arrived at his front door, that he didn't have his key. So he kneeled down on all fours on the lawn and began to search for the key.

Some of his students walked by. "Teacher, what are you doing?" they asked.

"I can't get in the house. I lost my key," he replied.

"Could we help you search for it?" the students inquired.

"Oh yes, thank you very much."

So, the students also got down on their hands and knees and, parting the blades of grass, searched for the key. After a couple of hours, one of the more assertive of the students turned to the professor and asked, "Do you remember where you last had that key?"

"Of course, I do," he responded, gruffly.

"Where?"

"In the house."

"Then why are you looking for it on the lawn?" the student asked.

"Well, it's much brighter out here."

I love this story, because it reminds us that so much of our spiritual quest is, in fact, about the kind of willful misdirection that marks our human condition. Like the professor, many of us would consider ourselves to be intelligent, even wise. We're loved by our friends, respected by our peers, and enjoy a certain professional success and material comfort. Yet, in the looking for the key to life's mysteries, we'll do everything we can to avoid searching in the place we *know* it is to be found. Instead, we'll spend much of our life minutely and intently examining where we know it *isn't* located, and engage others to help us in that fruitless task. Very few of us, cowed by those in authority— religious, secular, or both—will risk confronting the teachers of our faith traditions with the possibility that they're looking in the wrong place. And, when we do, we may find ourselves rebuffed or ridiculed for asking such an obvious question.

Of course, one reason why we spend so much of our lives turning over each blade of grass in an effort to seek the answer to our feelings of disconnection from the divine is that the truly hard work—the difficult, and even terrifying task of opening ourselves up to God—is a step into the unknown, into the darkness of that interior world that we'd much prefer to avoid, even though that's where the key is. So, we turn to the externals, the easily visualized show and form of faith, rather than sit in silence and await the darkness of God within the cloud of unknowing. I, like everyone else, was like the professor—all this time, searching for God in the light, where it was easier, instead of going deep inside myself and finding God there through centering prayer.

Developing a centering prayer practice wasn't easy for me. When I first started doing it, I had to go into the bathroom for complete privacy. I made sure I had a bathmat that was thick and fluffy and soft, so I could sit on the floor in between the bathtub and toilet and practice in peace. Sitting on the bathmat, I'd let my hands relax on my lap and my head rest without tension on my shoulders. I'd close my eyes and let a simple word come to me.

Abba.

Then I'd very gently say that word in my mind.

Abba.

Why *Abba*? As Thomas Keating observes, *Abba* is the word that Jesus himself uses to talk to God. *Abba*, he notes, is a child's word to describe the father—like 'Daddy.' *Abba* expresses our intimacy, dependency, and love. The word spoke to me, but it may not to others practicing centering prayer, and it's vital not to get hung up on which sacred words are 'appropriate' to use and which aren't. The meaning of the chosen word is not as important as the gentle, patient, refined way we return to it. It's not the content of the word that makes it sacred but its intent. Some people may be attracted to a word with a religious meaning such as *Abba*, *Jesus*, or *Amen*, one whose meaning itself facilitates the faith-response of turning towards God. For others, these same words may just stir up thoughts or anxieties about their religion and its various dogmas, or have other associations that prove distracting. Such people are better off using a neutral word like *Peace*. Because the sacred word by itself is only another thought, it too will need to be let go of—changed, refined, and dropped—until we rest in the silence. Indeed, as Thomas Keating says in

Open Mind, Open Heart, "The less the word means to you, the better off you are." Of course, thoughts will continually arise, and that is when we gently return to the sacred word, to focus our mind and concentration. God takes it from there.

In sum, centering prayer is the simple, patient, and repeated offering of ourselves to God. Whatever the thought—be it irritation at outside noise, consideration of the future, a memory of the past, an insight or idea, or even the sacred word itself—our natural action is to reflect on it and try to control it, reproduce it, or possess it. Instead, our aim, through the distillation of concentration that the sacred word brings about, should be to arrive at a peaceful, silent resting space: God's peace, which is a peace that surpasses understanding, reflection, and control. However, if we turn our minds onto that experience, it becomes *our* peace, not God's, and the peace is lost. When we return to the sacred word after reflecting on God's peace, we return it to its source: God. All we can do before God in centering prayer is to abandon humbly the turning and returning: turning toward Him by returning to the sacred word.

I'd practice centering prayer first thing in the morning. Before long, it became a means whereby I could get up and face the rest of the day. I would feel a sense of unity, as if I owned a reservoir of peace within me, I could draw upon. Usually by one in the afternoon, I'd be ready for the second session; if I missed it, it would show. Judith and Janet would say, "Oh, you didn't practice, huh?"

My daughters could see how much centering prayer was changing me. The opening to this transforming action of the Holy Spirit was beginning to deprogram the rage deep within me, which had been the dynamic in my life. My anger had always been just beneath my skin, and it never took too much for it to surface. Judith and Janet recognized that all too well. Essentially, the effect of centering prayer was the slow transformation of this anger into a willingness to be open and to receive whatever came my way.

Now, I cannot emphasize enough that none of this was easy. (After all, we don't stop being the professor on his hands and knees in the grass overnight. We've a lot invested in that distinguished and knowledgeable gentleman, and we enjoy being his faithful and dutiful students, parting the blades and looking for the key.) I assured myself that I would practice when I climbed out of bed in the morning and when I arrived home from work. I told myself I would sit before I prepared dinner. More often than not, however, come the morning I'd think, *I'll put on a pot of coffee first. I want to be awake when I do this prayer.* After I'd made the coffee, I'd take a shower, and then the next thing I knew, I'd be in the car on my way to work. I'd say, "Oh God! I forgot to do my prayer. But that's okay." (I loved talking to myself.) "When I get home this afternoon, I'll do it… Tomorrow morning, I'm going to do my prayer." For all my failings, I was never too hard on myself. I'd always say, "Well, you know what? My *intention* is God. Tomorrow, I'll double the amount."

Although I think it's important not to be judgmental about your spiritual practice (after all, who are you really punishing?), a practice is a practice—and as the old joke has it, "How do you get to Carnegie Hall? Practice, practice, practice." Like everyone engaged in any discipline, especially at the outset, I found it all too convenient to give myself special dispensation, last-minute waivers, and time off for good behavior. After all, it was *always* brighter outside! As it turned out, it took me nearly three years to be faithful to that 'twice a day, twenty minutes each time.'

My practice became even more important to me after Judith and Janet permanently moved out of the house. The year she graduated from her secretarial program, Janet married. Three months after Janet left home, Judith found a job in Manhattan as a caseworker for a foster care and adoption agency administered by Franciscan missionaries. She moved to a studio apartment twenty blocks away from work on West 65th Street. For a while, she'd been thinking about buying an apartment in the city or on Long Island and having me move in with her, but decided she needed her independence. It was probably for the best; the girls needed to get away from my overbearing presence.

With both my girls gone, I became very depressed. Empty-nest syndrome is hard for any parent to endure, and I believe that some of my bad behavior before the girls left was probably a case of my acting out of the fear, I had of being on my own again. It's hard for me to analyze my own feelings, precisely because I'm too close to them, but I won't rule out the possibility that I considered myself as forsaken as I had when my grandmother died, or when I found out I couldn't have biological children, or when my marriage broke down. That I tried to sabotage my own daughter's happiness—even at one-point commanding Janet to kneel when I heard that she was on the pill and forcing her to break off a previous relationship—tells me how deeply wounded I remained on matters of love, sex, and commitment.

I'm very grateful that throughout this difficult period in my life, my daughters and I nonetheless kept connected. Janet lived nearby and talked to me on the phone almost every day. She'd come over to help clean and cook meals, just as she had when she was in high school. As usual, I was working long hours at the hospital and always exhausted.

One day, I lay down to take a nap and fell into a deep sleep that lasted into the evening. I was rudely awakened by someone shaking me.

"Mom!" Janet yelled. "Why didn't you answer the door? Didn't you hear me calling you? Your skin is cold as ice. I thought you were dead!"

"Well, I'm not!" I yelled in return, just as angry at her for waking me up.

Looking back, I wonder, however, whether I was, in fact, dead. Or rather, something may have been dying in me—some aspect of my old life, my old patterns, that in turn expressed itself psychosomatically in my strange behavior. This too, might have been the work of centering prayer. As it is, it took me at least six months to get over the departure of my daughters from the home.

After Janet had been married for a year, she gave birth to a son, the first of her four children. Her husband went to computer school, and, having no income, the family was forced to apply for food stamps. I didn't give them any money. I would bring them a bag of groceries, and then I'd go home and cry. I felt sorry for my little grandson, but I didn't want to deprive the family of that pain, that growth that I considered our family had ultimately benefitted from. This really was tough love. I'd like to believe that it was necessary, but now I'm not so sure.

During this time, I didn't only rely on centering prayer for guidance in directing my spiritual life, but turned to other spiritual practices. Such ecumenism was very much in the spirit of the times. Indeed, in the wake of Vatican II, even the Roman Catholic Church had begun to encourage interreligious dialogue in those faiths (Buddhist, Hindu, and Christian) that had a monastic tradition. Thomas Keating and other monastics became deeply engaged in such dialogue, and were especially interested in understanding the differences and similarities between their approaches to non-conceptual meditation and prayer.

Even though I was a layperson, I too, wanted to know more about these practices. Before I became involved with the Separated and Divorced Catholics, I'd stayed by myself in the wilderness near Magog, Canada, in southeastern Quebec. I had a wonderful time, living in the forest with no one else around, and it certainly helped me gain some perspective on my discomfort at being alone. I pitched a small tent, made meals with my daughters' Girl Scout mess kit, and slept in a sleeping bag that couldn't keep the bugs out. I didn't speak to or see another soul for a week. I was scared, but I practiced how to deal with my fear.

My boss at Brunswick, Dr. David Hawkins, helped me learn about all different kinds of spirituality. The head of research at the hospital, Dr. Hawkins, was a well-known philosopher and scientist who worked on the Manhattan Project in the 1940s. He lived on Long Island's 'Gold Coast,' in a farmhouse made of imported stone and wooden beams from France, which Angelo and Connie Silveri later bought from him after his marriage ended. He ended up moving to Sedona, Arizona, and founded the Institute for

Spiritual Research. All this, and he was also related to the dashing sixteenth-century pirate, John Hawkins.

Dr. Hawkins and I had a genuine spiritual bond and an attraction. Many people who knew us thought something might have happened between us, had he not been married, and then remarried to a much younger woman. I was interested in everything he had to tell me. He especially liked giving me recommendations on what retreats to attend.

Once, on Dr. Hawkins' advice, I dragged Connie Silveri with me to a Buddhist monastery in upstate New York. We woke up at 4:30 A.M., meditated, ate breakfast, and then performed our chores. Connie was assigned to rake leaves while I cleaned the toilets. The work was agonizing—the old bursitis condition from my ironing flared up in my back and my knees pulsated with pain. But I was learning how to handle adversity.

Another time, Connie and I traveled upstate to do a Hindu cleansing. "This is a great thing, Mary, you should do it," Dr. Hawkins enthused. And so I did. When Connie and I arrived at the retreat, we were taken aback. In our high heels, we were definitely overdressed, and we were also the oldest people present. Everyone else looked like teenagers to us.

A Hindu monk showed us how to cleanse properly. This involved drinking eight glasses of salt water within half an hour. Trouble was, the facilities at the place couldn't accommodate this practice. We had to run out into the woods with a pail if we wanted to use the bathroom. After six days of this, Connie and I were exhausted and in agony. She was suffering from a massive migraine, while I was undergoing extreme abdominal pain. When I returned home, I passed a kidney stone. It took weeks for us to recover, during which we were instructed to eat only steamed vegetables. In fact, that was supposed to be our diet for the following four months. "Never again," Connie and I swore to each other.

But the cleanse did perform wonders. I lost weight and my skin glowed. I learned how closely the mind and body were connected. This wasn't something that was taught in the Catholic Church. We also learned how to focus properly. By the end of the retreat, we could have meditated in the middle of Times Square, so adept were we at tuning everything out.

By myself, I spent a week in a tent in the woods on Long Island. I'd been looking for a place to go to on my own, and Connie suggested her vacation home in Greenport, on the North Fork of Long Island. I camped on the property but never entered the house, even when it rained and my tent collapsed. At night, all the animals would emerge and I became quite good friends with them. Over the course of the week, I stopped caring about what my hair looked like, and my manicured nails were ruined. The neighbors must have thought I was a crazy person. In fact, someone did telephone Angelo to ask what I was doing on his lawn. It was difficult, but I stuck it out.

In addition, I tried Vipassana, Zazen, and a smorgasbord of other spiritual practices: some zany, some with merit. In taking part in them, I tried to remain open, even as I was also resistant to the full implications of what they involved. In some ways, I was following in the footsteps of the Indian prince, Siddhartha Gautama, who once stepped outside his gilded palace, saw the suffering that was all around him and spent years undergoing extreme asceticism and austerities in his efforts to get to the heart of the human condition. In the end, his realization under a pipal tree in Bodh Gaya—an awakening that changed his name to the 'Buddha'—was the Four Noble Truths and Eightfold Path based on the deep awareness of suffering. His path was the Middle Way, which rejected the notion that punishing spiritual practices would lead to enlightenment simply by being punishing. The Buddha saw that such self-denial can, perversely, be a way of reinforcing the self's identity—not solely because the practitioner may develop a kind of martyr complex or even foster damaging sadomasochistic impulses, but because such austerities might force the ego to fight back against its potential annihilation and the result might not be enlightenment but a full-blown psychic breakdown.

I'm very grateful for the time I spent exploring other religious practices. Even though I (and Connie) may have been out of place among the young would-be monastics and spiritual seekers, and we perhaps didn't take our obligations as seriously as we (and others) might have hoped, I certainly gained a respect for these traditions, especially in regard to how they showed you how to discipline your thought-processes and still the mind, which, as the Buddhist saying goes, jumps around like a monkey. In the end, however, I arrived at the conclusion that these traditions were not for me. Like centering prayer, Hindu and Buddhist practices also get you to a point of interior liberation, but the former is distinctive in that it brings you to the God of Abraham and Jesus. That's what I was looking for.

For all my participation in different faiths and in my attempts to foster the right kind of consciousness, I was nonetheless struggling with my centering prayer practice. It was just so hard to do it by myself. I complained and complained to Sr. Thelma Hall, until she finally threw up her hands in exasperation.

"Why don't you get a group together and do something about it?" she suggested.

"What do I do?" I asked.

"Just let people know that you're doing this prayer and what happens in your life. Tell them you'd like to get together, and then you do it."

As usual, Sr. Thelma was right. If anything, she showed me that I had to take responsibility for my spiritual journey.

I invited people I'd met from the Long Island Chapter of Separated and Divorced Catholics to join me in this new centering prayer group. The twelve of us would gather in my apartment on Sunday night, and afterward, I would serve an Italian supper. Part of the reason for the homemade food was to get people to come, especially the men. I realized that Sunday nights must be very lonely for a man separated from his family, and who might not have known how to cook. Our group needed to provide physical, as well as spiritual nourishment. We literally sat down and broke bread together.

We started meeting in the upper room of St. Brigid's Church in Westbury. Every time we gathered, we began with a contemplative walk, or walking meditation, in which you are mindful of the way in which the muscles are working in the body. The Vietnamese Buddhist monk, Thich Nhat Hanh, has long championed this method of concentrating the mind and body. Walking meditation acts as a kind of vestibule before one enters the sacred space. It's a means of quieting down, a way of coming to a center. Then we undertook two twenty-minute sessions of centering prayer. Sometimes, we ended with another contemplative walk.

I began holding centering prayer retreats for the group. We'd stay at a retreat house on Long Island, practice our prayer, and cook and have meals together, all in silence.

But nothing has come easily in my life, and I was still making every excuse to avoid going deeper into my spiritual practice. Again, I turned to Sr. Thelma during one of our spiritual guidance sessions.

"What should I do?" I asked.

"There's a centering prayer retreat being held next week in New Mexico," she disclosed. "It's with Fr. Keating."

It was the spring of 1983. A few months later, that retreat, and the man I would meet there, would change my life forever.

7 Faith

One day, when I was driving down a road near my home on Long Island, I saw a young man on a bike in the road in front of me. Coming up quickly behind me was a driver who seemed to be in a hurry. I slowed down so I wouldn't hit the bicyclist. However, the driver didn't see the bicyclist and started honking at me, trying to get me to move out of the way.

When I didn't, the driver sped up to pass me and rolled down his window. The obscenities that flew out of his mouth would make your ears blister! He even spat at me, narrowly missing my new spring hat.

This triggered all kinds of thoughts in my mind. *How could he do such a thing? What made him king of the road? How typical of a man, to think he was right about everything!*

In my head, I started cursing back at him, using language that was just as colorful. But I was aware that these negative thoughts were a dangerous path to take. I needed something to expel them from my mind, and keep me focused and centered.

I started to say my Active Prayer, two short sentences that would completely fill my mind.

Jesus, fill me with love and mercy. Jesus, fill me with patience.

After a while, my anger toward the driver was erased, and into that space rushed the Holy Spirit, telling me to forgive him. So I did, and that's how I discerned how strong and useful Active Prayer could be. I drove off down the road in a state of perfect peace and calm.

Fr. Keating liked to use this story to illustrate the power of Active Prayer.

I invoked an Active Prayer sentence constantly when I went to meet him, traveling nonstop for four days from Long Island to New Mexico in August, 1983. The only time I wasn't using Active Prayer was when I'd stop for the night at a motel. I'm sure many people thought I was crazy for taking a trip across the country to see a complete stranger in the hopes of spiritual enlightenment. But Sr. Thelma had convinced me that Fr. Keating was the teacher I was looking for.

Fr. Keating's two-week retreat took place at the Lama Foundation, a retreat center and community in San Cristobal, just north of Taos. Although Fr. Keating had held retreats before, including the one in Spencer, Massachusetts, which Sr. Thelma had attended, this was his first centering prayer retreat for laypeople.

The twelve attendees included individuals who would assume very important roles either in my life, or in the future of centering prayer. They included David Frenette, Bob Bartel, Fr. Carl Arico, Fr. Bill Sheehan, Bob Draper, and Gail Fitzpatrick-Hopler. I'd come to know many of these people better when Contemplative Outreach was formed. Two of them—David and Bob—I would get to know very well.

Bob Bartel was in his early thirties and had a background in Buddhism. David Frenette was in his late twenties. He'd grown up and gone to school in Michigan, after which he'd moved to Berkeley, California, since that was a hotbed of spiritual activity. He was originally drawn to Buddhism, but converted to Christianity. Then, at a lecture at Berkeley, he met Fr. Keating. Later, Bob mentioned to him that he was interested in becoming a monk. Fr. Keating suggested he try the two-week retreat in Lama to see how he liked contemplative living before making such a big decision.

Lama was not for the faint of heart. The conditions were primitive, with outhouses and solar-powered showers that could be as intermittent as the sunshine. The retreat lasted for two weeks and consisted of three parts. The first involved the teaching of centering prayer and meditation. The second consisted of morning and evening talks in which Fr. Keating presented the conceptual background behind those practices. Finally, during Mass, he used homilies to integrate the practice and conceptual background within a formal Christian setting. I'd never been exposed to this depth or intensity of spiritual thinking before, but it filled me with a kind of light I'd never known before.

All Fr. Keating knew about me was that I'd been recommended by Sr. Thelma. However, I think he was struck by how eager I was to go deeper into centering prayer. We hit it off right away—even though, or perhaps because, we were as different a pair as you could imagine. Although Fr. Keating was only three years older than me, and so we belonged to the same generation, our upbringing couldn't have been more different. We'd both been born in New York City, only I'd grown up among the Italian and Polish working-class in Jamaica, Queens, while he was born into a well-to-do family in Manhattan. I hadn't been allowed to finish high school, whereas he'd attended Yale and Fordham Universities. At the age of twenty, the age when I was about to get married, Fr. Keating entered the Trappist Order in Valley Falls, Rhode Island. Monastics take a vow of celibacy, poverty, and stability; and I'd only accomplished one of those—and my poverty was involuntary! We also were a physical contrast. I was five foot two in my stockinged feet and plump; he was well over six feet and angular, with the slight stoop that very tall people often develop as a result of bending down to talk to others or to avoid hitting their heads on lintels. I was brassy and blunt; he was (at least when I met him) polite and diplomatic. My hair was coiffed, my clothing was sharp, my nails were polished, and my heels were high; he was bald, his monk's outfit and sandals or shoes were well-lived-in and utilitarian, and I don't think he'd quite seen anything like me in his adult life!

For all my time in the world and his in the cloister, it was obvious to me from the outset that Fr. Keating had a sly sense of humor and an acute, even unnerving, eye for human foibles and the delusions with which we surround ourselves. I could say that I'd done the living and he'd done the praying, but that wouldn't be quite true. It was evident to me that years of being in community, including two decades as an abbot during a very turbulent time in the Catholic Church and in society at large, had cultivated in Fr.

Keating a shrewdness about the follies and vanities and vulnerabilities of human nature, as well as an appreciation for the various and sometimes surprising ways that the Holy Spirit can manifest itself. I think the fact that the Holy Spirit had brought me into Fr. Thomas' life was as surprising and instructive to him as Fr. Keating's presence in mine was to me.

Throughout the retreat, Fr. Keating would hold private interviews. When they were waiting their turn, the other attendees could tell whether I was the one meeting with him because they'd hear our laughter ringing out from behind the door. *That's Mary inside talking with him*, they'd think.

Once, I left an interview to bump into David Frenette waiting to see Fr. Keating. I couldn't hide the huge grin on my face as I winked at him. "Oh, you'll have such a good time," I assured David.

Fr. Keating and I didn't just talk about spiritual matters.

"What are you going to do with the rest of your life?" he asked me one day.

"I'll continue to work until I get my social security, and then I'll retire and spend time with my family," I replied, without much consideration.

"Oh, is that what you're going to do?" he inquired archly.

"I'm fifty-seven years old!" I protested.

"I thought maybe you might want to share the spiritual journey."

"Not really," I shot back. "That is, I don't really want to get into that stuff."

Fr. Keating looked very thoughtful. "What would it take to convince you to do it?"

I wasn't sure what he was proposing, but I decided to be honest, "A good-paying, part-time job."

"Really?"

"If someone offered me a good-paying, part-time job, I'd be willing to share centering prayer with other people."

That was the beginning and end of that conversation. However, the day before the retreat ended, Bob Draper walked up to me. He was from California and the president of National Health Laboratories. "Mary," he said. "I understand that if you had a good-paying, part-time job, you'd do some of the centering prayer work."

"I only mentioned that to Fr. Keating to shut him up," I complained, rather startled that my conversation was now apparently common knowledge. "I wasn't serious about that. As a single woman, I have to support myself."

Bob nodded, "I didn't mention this before, but I can make that happen. If you want a good-paying, part-time job, it's yours."

I still didn't take the offer very seriously. About a week after I returned home from the retreat, I received a phone call from Bob.

"Have you decided how much money you need?" was the first thing he asked.

"Please, I'm not going to do this kind of work," I replied. "I'm happy with my little centering prayer group. I really don't need anything."

The following week, Bob called again, and the week after that. Months passed, and I continued to refuse Fr. Keating's offer. It was kind of like a strange courtship. Or rather, the kind of message that the Holy Spirit kept on providing me with, and I kept refusing to accept it.

Then, on one of his visits to the East Coast, Fr. Keating came to see me.

"I understand you were offered a good-paying, part-time job," he said. "What is your answer?"

I'd insisted to Bob Draper that I wasn't interested in taking a job that involved centering prayer. But with Fr. Keating asking me in person, I had to reconsider. I was earning $60,000 a year at my medical administration job at Brunswick Hospital Center. I was only paying $200 a month in rent, living with my sister, Fran, and her family in Dix Hills on Long Island. I had a nice life.

Even if this job that Fr. Keating was proposing paid well and allowed me time to myself, how long would it last? Could I give up everything I'd worked for after my divorce and my daughters had left home? It seemed so risky.

Fr. Keating sensed that I was having trouble making a decision. "Maybe you should give it a little try," he suggested in that gentle, but firm manner that proved so persuasive.

My resistance collapsed. At Fr. Keating's request, I put together a brochure, which described centering prayer and offered advice on how to embark on a contemplative journey. I used my own personal knowledge and my recent familiarity with the Lama retreat. When Fr. Keating visited me again in a month, I showed it to him.

"What do you think?" I asked nervously. "Does it work?"

"Well, there's one correction," he smiled. "You spelled 'centering' wrong in the third paragraph."

So I took the good-paying, part-time job at the National Health Laboratories and started co-creating with Fr. Keating an organization called Contemplative Outreach.

* * *

Contemplative Outreach began when Fr. Keating was invited to assist a young man working out of Columbia University who wanted to establish a contemplative center and form a board of trustees. Fr. Keating recruited other people to the board, such as Gail Fitzpatrick-Hopler and Fr. Carl Arico, who'd both participated in the Lama retreat. Two other members, Edward Bednar (who actually thought up the name of the organization) and Gustave Reininger, disagreed over whether the center would be interreligious or exclusively Catholic, which would require the approval of the archbishop. The latter won out, and Ed Bednar left the board in early 1984.

The goal of Contemplative Outreach was—as it still is—to 'foster the process of transformation in Christ in one another through the practice of centering prayer.' As its first executive director, my task was to coordinate schedules, perform administrative work, and handle the bookkeeping. Since I'd been doing similar work as a medical administrator, this wasn't hard for me. The organization grew quickly.

I became close to many of the other board members, especially Gus Reininger. Gus led a sort of double life. In addition to being a scriptwriter in Hollywood for a number of successful television shows, such as *Crime Story* in the late 1980s, he was a deeply spiritual man who wrote extensively on centering prayer. We got along very well: he was my mystical brother and I was his mystical sister. Or, to put it another way, he represented my *animus*, the male archetype in my female unconscious, according to Jungian psychology.

Fr. Keating continued to come out from Colorado once a month to visit the Contemplative Outreach office, which was in the basement of Corpus Christi Church in New York City. The area in the early 1980s was very seedy and not somewhere you wanted to stay long. I'd drive in from Long Island on my few days a week, do my work, and then drive back out. Nonetheless, I always looked forward to Fr. Keating's visits. We had an undeniable connection, and everyone at Contemplative Outreach noticed it. Some people even called us 'soul mates.' Once, Fr. Keating showed me pictures of himself as a young man. It was hard to believe that this venerable man had ever been young, but here was the proof. "Oh, Tom, you were so handsome," I gushed, and he turned red. I always called him 'Tom.'

Despite the differences I've mentioned, Fr. Keating and I worked together very well. The Christian tradition contains many examples of men and women who come together to help shape spiritual teachings, such as Benedict and Scholastica, Francis of Assisi and Clare, John of the Cross and Teresa of Ávila, and Francis de Sales and Jane de Chantal. None of these were romantic couples, but they shared a spiritual bond and transcended their individual abilities by working as one. I certainly don't want to claim that we (or more especially I) were as accomplished as these spiritual titans, but we fit that same mold.

I like to think I brought a feminine element to the teaching of centering prayer that balanced his monastic mind and allowed centering prayer to reach a wider audience. Certainly, with our love and attention, it flourished. If Contemplative Outreach was the outward and public evidence of our spiritual relationship, inside and in private, Fr. Keating was helping my faith grow in a way I'd never thought possible. He taught me to consent, to allow God to direct me in my life. Through his instruction, I began to think about my spiritual journey as an adventure.

The analogy I like to use is that I'm an astronaut who climbs into a spaceship every day. I know that, as an astronaut, all I can do is watch the panels to make sure that everything is working. I watch the red and green lights go on, and I adjust my course. Occasionally, I get a little out of focus or I'm out of sync, but I make the corrections and then I'm on course again for this day. I don't direct the spaceship; NASA does, or rather, God. And I know in faith that the end of this adventure and journey is God's work. I've now come a very long way since Fr. Keating asked me what I planned to do with the rest of my life and I responded that I would work until I received my social security, and then retire and spend time with my family. Because of Fr. Keating, my spiritual journey took a fork in the road, toward the ultimate 'letting go' in life.

Part III Let Go

8 Commitment

I looked around the circle of women.

"Focus on something that happened to you this week," I said. "What were your emotions?"

"Anger," one of the women responded.

"Good, *anger*." I wrote the word down on a large piece of newsprint, "What are the other forms anger takes? What are the other feelings associated with anger?"

"Shame," another woman volunteered.

I wrote *shame* on the piece of paper. Writing these emotions down brought them to consciousness and helped them to be released later. This was the basis for one of the most popular workshops I taught on Long Island, called 'Release First and Letting Go,' in which I taught people to 'let go' of attachments. I'd been inspired by a workshop I'd attended for executives in Manhattan. The psychological technique impressed me and I thought I could translate it to the quest for an authentic and engaged spiritual life.

I already thought I had plenty of letting go. I'd let go of my marriage, my house, and my daughters. But I was far from finished: the hardest thing to let go of was myself.

Back in September, 1984, right after the Lama retreat, the gears were already turning for the establishment of what would become Chrysalis House, the lay contemplative community I'd live in for the rest of my life. After the retreat, I'd returned to Long Island, but some of the other attendees, such as David Frenette, Bob Bartel, and Pat Johnson, joined a nine-month experimental community located a mile away from Fr. Keating's monastery in Snowmass, Colorado. They conducted retreats there based on the Lama experience and Fr. Keating's work. I was asked to be on their board of advisors.

In summer, 1985, Fr. Keating asked me if I wanted to start a new live-in community with David and Bob on the East Coast. He considered it important that the community be located on the East Coast since so many people in that part of the country had become interested in centering prayer, much of which was due to what we'd accomplished with our prayer groups in the area.

For a long time, I'd dreamed of starting a retreat house for laywomen, as a place where women could live a spiritual life. What Fr. Keating was proposing wasn't that different. Nonetheless, I was full of trepidation. I thought to myself that I had to be to be insane to agree. How could I give up everything in my life to go live in a place with two other people I didn't even know? I was fifty-nine years old. David and Bob were in their late twenties and early thirties. What could they possibly know about life?

I thought, *This is not possible, God, but I'll do it.*

David and Bob flew out to New York, I picked them up from LaGuardia Airport, and we drove to look at a potential location in northwest Connecticut. A couple who'd attended a retreat at Snowmass was offering us their farmhouse, located on forty acres, near the town of West Cornwall. We agreed to rent it, and so in September, 1985, David, Bob, and I prepared to live there for a year.

This stage of my life would require another form of letting go—one potentially full of pitfalls. I had to resign from my job at Brunswick Hospital Center, where I'd been working for the past decade. I'd never considered my job to be a career or something that filled all my needs. It certainly allowed me to support myself and pay the bills, and, as with every task, I made sure that I worked to the best of my ability. But this was nevertheless a major change. In fact, my friend and colleague, Barbara, was upset and took my resignation personally. Barbara had learned to rely on my support and friendship, and she couldn't understand why I'd want to give up my job for a life of contemplation. But I recognized I had to follow my own path.

After Angelo and Connie Silveri had sold their house in Plainview and relocated to my old boss, Dr. Hawkins' house in Upper Brookville, I'd moved in with my sister, Fran, in Dix Hills. I'd still managed to keep many of my possessions. Now I let them all go: Judith received my fine teacup sets, my Tiffany lamps went to Fran, and Janet took ownership of my Ethan Allen furniture. I also asked my friends from my centering prayer group to choose the furniture and crystal they wanted. "Take them," I said. For someone who'd felt such pride in being able to afford the finer things in life—one my parents hadn't been able to afford for us—the voluntary relinquishing of my material possessions was a major step forward in my spiritual growth. I surprised myself in how completely I entered into the spirit of that renunciation.

What was truly hard was leaving my children. Even though I was not entering into a formal monastic arrangement, I was, nonetheless, expected to dedicate myself wholly to the house and that would necessarily mean I'd not be as available to Janet and Judith as I had been before. I was being not just physically, but emotionally separated from Judith and Janet. They felt worse, and wondered whether I'd replaced them with two child surrogates, David and Bob, who were about the same age as the girls. My absence from their lives had real consequences that were more painful than I perhaps realized at the time. Once, Judith was experiencing a bad breakup with a boyfriend and couldn't confide in me because I away on a retreat. I hoped they understood how important they were in my life, even if I was no longer was available to them as I used to be.

On a visit to the house in West Cornwall, Judith turned to me, "I know it's good for everyone to have you in this new community, but who will challenge you, Mother?" She needn't have worried. The first year in West Cornwall presented us with real disputes. David, Bob, and I lived simply, with no salaries but room and board. At first, we didn't have health insurance. We received a stipend of $100 a month, but that amount was barely enough to cover gas for the car. For the initial few months, we fixed up the house, and then started offering weekend and ten-day retreats, as well as weekend introductions to centering prayer. Many of the people who took part were those who'd joined me for my prayer groups and workshops.

I was also challenged by the fact that although I was the administrator for the community, I had to give up being in charge. Unlike David and Bob, I'd lived a full life before coming to West Cornwall. I'd been a businesswoman and a spiritual group leader. I'd been married and divorced, and I'd raised two daughters. I was a grandmother. So, it was tough for me to let go of my former identity and my ever-present need to control any situation.

An incident that first year in West Cornwall reinforced for me the importance of letting go. The house had a large wood stove that heated part of it, including the meditation room. David, Bob, and I took turns stoking the fire with logs. One day, I lost my balance trying to stoke and severely burned my upper lip on the lid of the stove. My lip turned bright red and inflamed. When I strode into the kitchen to meet David and Bob for our tea break, they stared at me, horrified.

"Mary, what's wrong?" David asked.

"It's nothing, I burned my lip," I muttered, even though it was painful for me to speak. I went to the cabinet where we kept our first aid kit, "I just need some balm."

"I think you need to go to the hospital," Bob ventured to say.

"Please, Mary, let us take you to a doctor," David agreed.

But I didn't want to go to a doctor. Ever since I'd been a young woman, when that drugged-out doctor had cut me up, I didn't trust the medical profession. So, I practiced my 'letting go and release' of this pain. Against David and Bob's wishes, I drove by myself to the local pharmacy in town. The only people there, were a young college student staffing the register and the pharmacist who sat behind her on his elevated platform.

I walked up to them. "Do you have a natural remedy for burns?" I asked.

The college student stared at me, clearly shocked and thinking that I needed something stronger. The pharmacist, who didn't bother looking up from what he was doing, mumbled, "Take a look on the third rack on the left aisle of 3C."

"Wait," the college student squeaked, but I flew off to get the natural remedy.

When I returned home, I applied this balm to my lip. By the end of three days, it had completely healed. Not only did I take this as a demonstration of the power of letting go, but I saw it as a sign that I was finally shedding my self-image, my old self.

As that first year progressed in West Cornwall, David, Bob, and I encountered further challenges. Making a commitment was easy—we all made formal commitments to each other in writing to Fr. Keating that we'd live in this community for one year, which we agreed would be sufficient time to determine whether such an arrangement was possible. What was genuinely difficult was making decisions, since everything was reached by consensus. If consensus couldn't be reached, we consulted Fr. Keating during his monthly visits out east.

That first year, we spent four to five months debating whether there should be a celibacy rule. Bob didn't feel called to celibacy, whereas David was living a monastic life but wanted openness for the future. I thought it would be most practical if we had a rule. Of course, I'd been married before and wasn't a young man like David and Bob, with their lives and possibly children ahead of them.

Finally, we asked Fr. Keating, and he made it clear to us that he thought a commitment to celibacy was important as a way of focusing our intentionality and ensuring a degree of communal cohesion. So, at the end of that first year, Bob decided the community wasn't for him and left. (Later, David introduced Bob to a female friend, and the two married.) The live-in community was down to two people.

David and I had hoped to stay at our location in West Cornwall for another year, but after that first year was up, the couple who rented it to us informed us they wanted it back. Fortunately, Angelo and Connie offered to let us stay in their vacation home in Greenport while we found a new location. We ended up in Greenport for nine months, during which time we continued to host retreats but were unable to really settle down.

Then one day, David was scanning the rentals section of the *New York Times*. He found a place in Warwick, New York, about fifty miles north of New York City. We ended up staying in this house on Ball Road for four years. Following the first year in West Cornwall, after Bob had departed, both David and I maintained we should extend our one-year commitment to three. We made our three-year formal commitment right before we obtained the three-year lease for the house in Warwick. Obviously, this was a sign that we'd arrived at the right decision.

The Ball Road house was perfect for our purposes, except it was rather small. Our retreats were growing, and the place only had room for twelve to fourteen people. When they came, they had to sleep in the basement or three to four in a room.

All this time, we hadn't given the community a proper name. Then one night, the name 'Chrysalis House' appeared to me in a dream. I saw a caterpillar weave a chrysalis around itself, and then emerge as a beautiful butterfly. I woke up with the thought that this community was exactly like a chrysalis. People could come here and be shaped and formed by spiritual teachings. Then they'd fly away as a freer and truer version of themselves. It was the ultimate metamorphosis. Thomas Keating explicitly connected this evolution to the abandonment of the false self: "Chrysalis House is designed to be a place of purification and transformation, where the skin of the false self is gradually shed and the new person in Christ is formed."

Many people whom I'd known on Long Island and who'd followed me to the house in West Cornwall also stayed at Chrysalis House. One such person was Cathy McCarthy, who'd lived in a convent for six years and attended my retreats on Long Island. When we first met, Cathy reckoned she had a solid spiritual background but wanted to develop the human element to her practice, which she thought I embodied. She divulged to me that when she'd first seen me speak, she'd reflected to herself, *This woman has what I want, and I want what she has.* Cathy joined Chrysalis House as a permanent member in 1988, starting with two six-month commitments.

Another member, Mary Dwyer, joined in September, 1990. Mary was in her early thirties, from a Jesuit background, and a former banker. When she first met me, I'd just returned from a retreat. I was wearing a black cocktail dress and black high heels. I had on blue eyeshadow, mascara, and jewelry, and my nails (as usual) were long and painted red. In contrast, Mary wore Birkenstocks and her hair was cut short. I knew my appearance must have shocked her—she must have expected someone who looked more like a nun. But I enjoyed being smartly dressed and wasn't about to give up that part of my identity. I was well versed in how to arrange my clothes, and I was always changing my hair color. After all, butterflies could be eye-catching and full of color!

Like most people who joined Chrysalis House, Mary Dwyer entered the community with certain expectations about life. She disclosed to me once that she'd been deeply disillusioned. I looked at her, "Thank God. How would you have known you had so much illusion?" I think this helped her, even after she left Chrysalis House in 1992, to earn a Master's degree in social work.

At the time Mary Dwyer joined, the three-year lease at Ball Road had almost expired and we needed to find a new location for Chrysalis House. Fortunately, a property opened up for sale across town on Bellvale Lakes Road that was perfect. It was on twelve wooded acres and consisted of three houses put together, with a residence for five people, three kitchens, a wing that could accommodate twenty-five people, and a chapel. It had formerly been a convent to ten Carmelite nuns.

The problem was that the nuns wanted $800,000 for the place, a considerable sum in 1990. The Silveris agreed to buy a house for me. We asked Fr. Keating to come east and talk to the nuns, to show them that we weren't some strange cult and were serious about our commitment.

That night, I prepared a turkey dinner for Fr. Keating, which was his favorite. David, Cathy, and I had just presented him with our formal five-year commitments. As we were sitting down to dinner, the doorbell rang. It was our real estate agent, who'd come to tell us that the nuns had accepted our offer of $500,000. The nuns must have been very impressed by Fr. Keating. But we didn't learn the news until *after* we'd made our five-year commitments. This was yet another sign that we were on the right path.

In our new location on Bellvale Lakes Rd., Chrysalis House flourished. Our daily schedule was as follows:

- 5:00 A.M.: Arise.
- 5:30 A.M.: Come together for one hour of centering prayer.
- 7:00-9:00 A.M.: Quiet time; pick up your own breakfast.
- 12:00 P.M.: Come together for thirty minutes of centering prayer.
- 1:00 P.M.: Common meal with conversation and companionship.
- 2:00 P.M.: Household chores such as cleaning, laundry, gardening, etc.
- 5:30 P.M.: Come together for one hour of centering prayer, then pick up your own supper.
- 7:00 P.M.: Solitude and silence until morning.

Half the time, our schedule followed the normal routine; the other half consisted of retreats. I would also meet with people for individual spiritual guidance. After a weekend retreat, we'd spend Monday morning cleaning up, and after lunch, we'd have free time until Tuesday night. This was our time off. We'd go separately for a hike, or into town, or take the bus into the city. Sometimes, I'd visit my relatives. We'd all be back by Tuesday night and the schedule would start again. This arrangement was as structured as any religious community.

Although for the most part life at Chrysalis House ran smoothly, issues still arose. We debated on whether to make permanent vows (we ended up deciding against it), and whom we'd allow to join as residents. Usually, our community would include three permanent members at a time, and sometimes as many as five. I thought some of the rules were petty, like not allowing TVs in the bedrooms. Also, some rooms were more accommodating and better decorated than others; for example, I slept in a cold room in the basement.

Money was always tight, even though I donated to Chrysalis House the funds that I received whenever I presented a talk or workshop outside of the community. By this stage, I was being asked to speak not only nationally, but internationally—Europe, Mexico (which I loved because it was so green), and the Dominican Republic. Others in the community resented the fact that I was often away for long periods of time and wondered if I could fulfill my duties. But truthfully, I was the breadwinner of the group.

At times, I felt that the other members of Chrysalis House didn't appreciate me or think of me as one of them. Occasionally, they'd forget to include me in their social activities. One year, we held a retreat at Easter time, and the house was full. On the last day, many of the attendees hung around, wanting me to give them spiritual guidance. David, Cathy, and Mary didn't wait and went out to Easter dinner without me. When they returned, they found me lying on the couch watching old movies. Maybe it was hard for them to remember that I was a person who needed companionship. Maybe it was hard for me, still, to let go of old patterns of wanting to be noticed and appreciated.

With the input of the other residents, I developed the Welcoming Prayer, inspired by the mystics and the eighteenth-century French priest, Jean-Pierre de Caussade's *Abandonment to Divine Providence.* De Caussade speaks of 'letting go so that we may see and know God and His will.' He tells us to look beyond piety and to release into the present moment. "What God arranges for us to experience at each moment is the best and holiest thing that could happen to us," he says. "You seek perfection and you meet all that happens to you. All you suffer, all you do, all your inclinations are mysteries under which God gives himself to you while you are vainly straining after high-flown fancies." This was the foundation of the Welcoming Prayer, which we used in the Open Mind Open Heart Workshop, which I also developed based on Thomas Keating's book of the same name.

The Welcoming Prayer is a radical departure from the world of resentment, self-righteousness, and judgment—a world of duality where right and wrong, good and bad rule our consciousness. To welcome and let go is one of the most radically loving, faith-filled gestures we can make in each moment of each day. It's a call to the higher rather than the lower—an open-hearted embrace of all that is in ourselves and in the world.

Like centering prayer, the way to understand the Welcoming Prayer is to do it, because it's absolutely illogical and irrational. First, you notice and sink into the feelings, emotions, thoughts, sensations, and commentaries in your body. Secondly, you accept the fact that what you're experiencing also contains the divine by simply saying, "Welcome." Thirdly, you adopt an attitude of surrender by inwardly affirming the following intention: "I let go of the desire for security, affection, and control. I let go of the desire to change the situation."

Security, affection, control. These needs have marked my life, as they mark the lives of all of us to a greater or lesser extent. They form some of the programs for happiness that Thomas Keating observes are the constructions of the false self. These are the most difficult aspects of ourselves to let go—not least because we've invested the entire course of our life in maintaining, strengthening, and justifying them. We possess a mind that tells us that we're always right and everybody else is wrong. Our emotions validate these thoughts, and look for ways to affirm them continually. The practice of centering prayer has a tendency 'to evacuate spontaneously the undigested emotional material of a lifetime, opening up a new space for self-knowledge, freedom of choice,' as Thomas Keating writes in *An Invitation to Love*. The objective in the Welcoming Prayer is to let go of whatever is happening on an interior level and surrender, so that we can see reality and what is *actually* happening, instead of perceiving through our thoughts and feelings what we want to occur.

At Chrysalis House, we used the Welcoming Prayer all the time in our daily lives. For instance, I employed it often in my interactions with Cathy McCarthy, as I'm sure she did with me. Cathy and I were similar in a lot of ways. We were both in our mid-to-late fifties, were gregarious and enjoyed the company of people, and were utterly strong-willed. To me, Cathy had invaded my space; Cathy practiced everything she was going to say to me, but when she did it, I never reacted in the way she expected. Nearly every day, we challenged each other. For a while, I was Cathy's spiritual director, but I stopped because I realized it wasn't fair, given our relationship. She couldn't very well talk about her problems with me and expected me to give her guidance. I think she just wanted my approval too much.

Despite our differences, it's clear to me now that Cathy was my greatest gift. Usually, when we say that someone is a 'gift,' we mean that that person is a real trial in our lives. But sometimes, the difference is not actually a distinction. Cathy made me realize that whatever problems you're having with someone, it's never about the other person. It's about what *you're* feeling inside; your own experience.

Once, I was scheduled to speak in London, England, while Cathy was hosting a retreat at Chrysalis House. I was sitting down at the table with David and Cathy, when the latter turned to me. "We have a lot of people signed up for this retreat and nowhere for them to stay," she noted. "Do you mind if someone stays in your room while you're away?"

I was so filled with rage that I couldn't even think. David and Cathy looked at each other as if to say, *What's wrong with her now?*

"Excuse me for a moment," I murmured. I stood up and walked into another room.

I focused on my feelings of rage and slowly welcomed them. *Welcome. Welcome.*

I let go of my desire to control the situation. I let go of my desire to change what was happening. *Welcome. Welcome.*

Gradually, my head cleared, and in that space left by my feelings of anger and helplessness, I realized why I'd been so infuriated by Cathy's request. I was back to being a child at the house on Shore Avenue, in Queens. I'd had my own room until I was seven years old. Then, my sister was born, and from then on, I'd had to share my room. The idea of allowing a stranger to sleep in my room had triggered that raw, unprocessed, childish reaction from me. That need for security, affection, and control had been awakened, and vehemently.

I took a deep breath and returned to David and Cathy. "I don't know if you noticed just now," I said to them, "but I had to go out of the room so I could do the Welcoming Prayer."

They both laughed, and I laughed with them. My feelings had been so transparent.

Then I turned to Cathy, "Of course you can have someone stay in my room while I'm gone."

And I meant it too. Before I left for my trip, I prepared my room for a guest. I cleaned it, made space in the drawers and closets for their clothes, and put a bouquet of flowers in it. I had turned a childhood trauma into a positive benefit for someone else and given myself a small gift of peace.

When Thomas Keating had suggested that I help to form Chrysalis House, he perhaps may only have been thinking logistically—that I lived on the East Coast and an obvious demand existed for centering prayer retreats. When he asked us to make a formal commitment to living in community, as part of our ongoing institutional commitment to Contemplative Outreach, he was perhaps thinking solely that it would be worth determining whether a lay community dedicated to living out, as well as teaching, centering prayer would be possible and this process required some time to figure itself out.

But I've always wondered whether the Holy Spirit didn't guide us to a more profound space with the founding of Chrysalis House. When I facetiously blurted out that I'd accept a well-paid, part-time position, I really had no idea that I'd be taken seriously. And when I repeatedly informed Thomas Keating that I had no intention of entering any kind of religious community, I genuinely had no conscious expectation that, shortly thereafter, I would do precisely that. Yet, the Holy Spirit discerned my inner work was not yet complete. Since my childhood, my home life had been fraught with physical danger and emotional difficulty; as a mother, I'd been controlling and concerned to maintain an outward front of material success and achievement to cover up the torment that I frequently found myself undergoing. I'd been divorced from the House of God, both metaphorically and in my marital status.

It was clear that, at some very deep level, I needed to refashion a home where I could be fully myself as a spiritual practitioner, without fear of ridicule from my family or threat of violence. I needed to create a safe space for those younger than I, and who were, to an extent, dependent on me as a breadwinner. And I needed a space where I could breathe air into my inner life—after a lifetime of pressing and ironing and flattening out my deepest desires (and those of others) to conform to the expectations placed upon me as a girl, a woman, a wife, a mother, a person of faith, and a fully realized human being.

In Chrysalis House, I was once again a mother—this time to Bob and David, as well as to the other retreatants. Once again, I was challenged with my wish to control and to shape the lives of those around me. I was being called every day to challenge my false self's desperate wish to be indispensable, to be of service to God, and to be the kind of pious and passive Catholic girl my grandmother expected me to be, and that was deeply tied to my self-identity as a do-gooding, discarded, and unloved rescuer of the discarded and unloved. It was as if the Holy Spirit, through Thomas Keating, comprehended that the best person to form Chrysalis House would always be the most wounded of the healers; that the *psyche* (the Greek word for 'butterfly') that required the longest pupation would be the most appropriate soul to help others take flight; that the person who'd struggled all her life to match her interior wishes and aspirations to be close to God with the daily obligations of looking after others would find herself deeply embedded in community, fostering both.

A famous Zen proverb runs, "After enlightenment, the laundry." It's a saying that anyone who's lived in an intentional community with an intensive spiritual practice will know very well. The proverb obviously intends to nurture humility in all practitioners, as well as suggest that

165

living in community still continues, even after the ultimate revelation. But it also wants us to recognize that daily activities, even as dull and repetitive as washing the laundry, offer their own spiritual lessons—perhaps as life-changing and soul-penetrating as enlightenment itself. Of course, I'd spent a good many years ironing other people's clothes in the basement, as well as attempting as a single mother to look after my children's welfare. I had not, as I recognized very well, approached these tasks with the mind of an enlightened being! But who's to say that the ironing had not, in its own way, prefaced the spiritual insights I'd been afforded?

I also think that the proverb wants to draw attention to the extra challenges that face spiritual seekers living in community. Thomas Keating has observed of the monastic life and the false self that unless you work on changing the false self, simply changing your physical location or the company you keep won't alter those deep patterns. Instead of drinking your friends under the table as a means of expressing your identity, you will fast the other monks under the table instead. Sure, you may outwardly appear different, even spiritual, but your compulsive, narcissistic, and self-aggrandizing delusional behavior will remain the same.

Chrysalis House, therefore, offered a further way of living the Zen proverb: coping with the foibles of spiritual seekers living in community. I was no different from others in bringing my deeply wounded self into close companionship with others who shared the human condition with me. We all brought our preconceptions of what an intentional community should feel like, and our presumptions about what it meant to be a 'spiritual' person. Living in community, however, offers you no place to hide. Even the most diligently self-deluded individual will eventually reveal their false (and most tightly held) self to those with whom they live. And when you are collectively engaged in a common pursuit to live more authentically, oriented toward a common goal, that identity can explode with that much more force. 'After enlightenment, the laundry,' therefore, reminds us that the daily rounds of taking care of the center, looking after the bookings and the finances, and simply maintaining the property, are a way of stabilizing the self and ensuring that the 'enlightenment' part is itself disciplined.

So, Chrysalis House distilled the proverb to its essence, because our entire lives in that residence were directed to finding enlightenment in the laundry, and laundry in the enlightenment. We were all in service to God, in every aspect of our lives, and through centering prayer we were, at heart, attempting to welcome and forgive all of what it took to be alive to creation.

As difficult as it was, living in Chrysalis House allowed me to make a commitment to an intimate relationship with God. Everything you did there, everything you underwent, was part of your commitment, and I never found it binding. I'd never thought before about what the word *commitment* meant. 'Commitment' points toward engagement with and activity over a long period. The word *wholeheartedness* points toward a depth of engagement at a given moment in time. Commitment is a vertical engagement and wholeheartedness is horizontal. Regarding work, we focus on one project at a time, and do it wholeheartedly, giving it our full attention. When we engage in it for a long time, it becomes commitment. Faith is connected to commitment, for what we call *discipline* is really faith. Faithfulness is what keeps us on the spiritual journey, and keeps us going when our wholeheartedness begins to wane.

Some people say that I gave up everything for the contemplative life. But what I relinquished was nothing in comparison to what I received. I received everything. I learned to be open; to become a vessel, an instrument. I learned what it truly means to make a commitment to a life in the spirit.

9 Forgiveness

When I was a child, my parents fought. I could hear my father knocking my mother to the ground, and slamming her to the wall. I'd gather up my brothers and sister and rush them upstairs into a bedroom so they'd be safe. Then, when I was married, my husband and I would argue. We didn't hit one another, but we abused each other verbally and furniture was thrown. My children would go outside and rush to a neighbor's house to escape the yelling. It's a source of shame to me that I wasn't able to change the patterns in my own relationship that I undergone with my parents'. Years later, while at Chrysalis House, I found myself at a maximum-security prison every week, where potential violence completely surrounded me. It wasn't easy at first, but what I gained from living this way was more than I could have imagined.

I started my involvement with the prison ministry at Eastern Correctional Facility in Wawarsing, New York, in 1992. The prison was located around thirty miles north of Warwick, and was one of the oldest penal institutions in the state—at the time I visited, it was almost a hundred years old. Every time I drove up Route 209, I'd find myself stunned as the building rose into sight. It literally looked like a cloister or a castle, with four turrets and a copper roof turned green by oxidation, set against a backdrop of mountains.

I led a prayer group once a month, from 6:30 to 8:30 in the evening, in a room off St. Jude's Chapel—a resonant place for me, given my personal history with lost causes and the name of my elder daughter. Getting into the prison was difficult. There were multiple checkpoints and guards who asked you questions. Finally, I'd walk down the main hall and into a room off the chapel. In front of the green-carpeted stage sat twenty-five men, all hardened criminals, waiting for me to say something.

"Welcome, welcome," I greeted. "Today, we'll be talking about how to be free."

The men looked doubtful.

"I know you don't believe me," I continued. "But it's in the freedom—the freedom to become holy—that you get the opportunity to fall in love, so that you can live any place in the universe, with anyone."

They still observed me skeptically. I didn't blame them. What did I know, this woman in her red suit and gold jewelry?

I liked to dress up whenever I spoke in front of an audience, no matter who they were. I did this on a limited budget too. I especially liked to dress up if the audience was all men, not just at the prison, but at the Seminary of the Immaculate Conception in Huntington on Long Island. The seminarians thought I was just another nun coming to talk, but little did they know. I'd stand in front of them in my high heels, makeup, and long, red, manicured nails and talk about things the faculty there didn't want to touch: sexuality and intimacy. I emphasized that it was okay to have sexual feelings, that *eros* was as God-given as *philia* (brotherly and sisterly affection) and *agape* (divine love). I even compared my relationship with God to an orgasm, that every inch of my body was electrified by the love of God. Needless to say, the seminarians were shocked, but I didn't care.

At the risk of being salacious or merely trite, I believe my association with Thomas Keating contained an erotic component. It is an essential facet of the Christian faith that it is an incarnate religion. Indeed, many decades of the period between Christ's death and the Council of Nicaea in 324, were taken up with arguing precisely over the bodily status of the Christ and its relationship with the Trinity, with, ultimately, those who claimed the non-corporeality of God in Jesus losing the argument. Catholic spirituality has long recognized the importance of sexuality within the human person. The vows of chastity within marriage and celibacy within holy orders are not efforts to deny human sexuality, but to transform its power into the broad meaning of *caritas*, or love, for all humankind.

Indeed, I don't see how erotic attraction can be excluded from human spirituality; in fact, attempting to bury, ignore, or somehow resent the presence of that aspect of our being human only leads to distortion or emotional stultification or incontinence. *Eros* doesn't need to be acted upon but it is, I believe, a mistake to pretend it wasn't a part of us. So, I certainly have no qualms in admitting to enjoying my sexuality and being a spiritual seeker—and fully enjoying the wisdom of both. I firmly believe that acknowledging the force and dynamism of our sexuality is essential if the spiritual practitioner is to remain a whole person.

Therefore, when I talk about *eros*, I'm actually thinking much more broadly and deeply than simply physical attraction, arousal, or even touching or being touched by another person. The *eros* that I mean is a creative force that disrupts old patterns of behavior and relationship and creates new ones. *Eros* disturbs and enlivens, energizes and destabilizes. Too often, in our rush toward the physical satisfaction of the more superficial dimensions of erotic attraction, we stifle the truly transformational power of this life-giving force. Because a physical relationship between Fr. Keating and myself was not possible, I believe, that deeper erotic component could be allowed to flourish. Indeed, Contemplative Outreach is partly the result of that connection.

In fact, when I'd first started at Contemplative Outreach, the basement of Corpus Christi Church, where our offices had been, had contained a file cabinet with the journals of Thomas Merton, who'd been baptized at nearby St. John's Cathedral. I couldn't help but dip into them and read some of Merton's most intimate entries. At one point, he talked about his tormented love for a student nurse, Margie, describing every detail of her hair and lips with tenderness and passion. I was stunned at this revelation, but I wasn't really surprised, and certainly not judgmental about how Merton, who'd been lauded as the perfect monastic, had found himself profoundly shocked by his sudden exposure to erotic love. In the two remaining years of his life, his humanity and, indeed, his spiritual practice had deepened as a result of his profoundly disturbed investigations of the erotic's place in the divine plan for him.

For all of that, I didn't feel it was fair to discourse at length about *eros* in the prison ministry, but you could detect a sensual current between the inmates and me. When they became used to me, they started calling me 'The Lady.' "When's The Lady coming?" they'd ask. "I need to see The Lady." Whenever I arrived, an announcement was made over the P.A. system: "The Lady just arrived." The inmates described me as 'connected,' 'outgoing,' and 'impeccably dressed.' Some even declared that I lived 'the complete life.'

We had a strong connection, the inmates and I, even though many of them were in prison for murder. One prisoner, named Dan, was inside for six years for slitting his wife's throat; others must have committed much worse crimes, because they were in for life. I didn't know these men's offenses, but that wasn't important. What was, was that they were open to living differently than they'd ever lived before.

"Do you want to be right or do you want to be free?" I liked to ask people. (Of course, I always had to be right; I thought that was how I would gain people's approval!) This saying, I concluded, applied most to these inmates. They needed to forgive in order to be truly free, and I wanted to show them that we all have the power to forgive. This power was given to us through the Pentecost, I told the inmates, when Jesus said, "If you forgive the sins of any, they are forgiven; if you retain the sins of any, they are retained" (John 20:23). He knew it would free us, so He gave us the responsibility to forgive: "Judge not, and you will not be judged; condemn not, and you will not be condemned; forgive, and you will be forgiven" (Luke 6:37). The Church,

I observed, performed the sacrament of reconciliation or confession, but that was usually directed by the top three inches of our head. It wasn't deep within us, and it wasn't reaching that realm where the spirit dwells. We had to enter into the bosom, into the heart, I added, into the sacred place. That was where it was possible to do the Forgiveness Prayer.

The first time I walked the inmates through the Forgiveness Prayer, many of them were uncomfortable because they were experiencing intense emotions. I provided them with a cassette tape for them to practice in their cells, so that after they'd completed centering prayer, they could move on to the Forgiveness Prayer. That provided them with some support until I visited them the next month.

On the tape, they heard me say:

First, you take some deep breaths and begin to focus. Take your mind's eye, the intuitive eye, and bring your attention to the top of your head and begin to relax your scalp.

Relax. Relax.

Bring your focus to your inner eye, and begin to relax the muscles of your face. Allow your tongue to float in your mouth, not touching the roof of your mouth or the floor of your mouth. Just let it float there, to bring your body, mind, and spirit into balance. Bring your attention to your throat area.

Relax. Relax.

Take your inner eye and bring your focus to the back of your neck, your shoulders, upper arms, and lower arms, letting them hang loose. Bring your attention to your upper back and relax the muscles up and down your spine. Then to your buttocks and abdomen, and relax those muscles.

Relax. Relax.

Bring your focus and attention to your thighs and relax those muscles, past the knees and the calves, letting the stress and discomfort leave your body through your toes.

Then, bring your focus and attention to your chest area. Let that light move in a circular motion around your bosom, resting open. Then it enters your bosom and you move through a passageway that is warm and dark and safe.

At the end of the passageway is a doorway, filled with light. Give yourself permission to move through the light and the doorway into a meadow that is filled with light and sunshine, and a soft breeze that just moves across your face. Using all your senses, move down this pathway, allowing the sun to warm you on the path to your sacred place. Enter into this sacred place and rest in the bosom of the spirit, allowing yourself to be held and to be nurtured.

In just a few moments, a person will appear, and when that person appears, invite the person into your sacred place. Use the person's name. Allow that person to enter into your sacred place. Begin to share with the person how you have been hurt and traumatized. Be very specific in sharing your feelings, your thoughts, and your experience of how you have been hurt and your relationship with this person. Now tell the person that you forgive them.

I forgive you. I forgive you. I forgive you.

Now ask the person how you have offended the person, hurt and traumatized the person. *How have I hurt you?* Wait for an answer. *How have I offended you?* Ask for forgiveness.

Forgive me. Forgive me. Forgive me.

Allow the person to leave your sacred place. If the person needs to return, allow the person to leave as you continue to rest in the bosom of the spirit of the grace of God. Prepare to leave your favorite and sacred place. Feeling refreshed, move down the path towards the door filled with light, and give yourself permission to move through the doorway into the passageway. Move into the chamber of your heart in the bosom and allow yourself to emerge into normal state of consciousness, slowly and safely. When you're ready, open your eyes.

When I came on my monthly visit, some of the inmates confessed to me that they had trouble with the Forgiveness Prayer.

"When I go down into this sacred space, all these people line up that have to come in," one man complained. "I don't know which one to choose, and then before you know it, it's over and I haven't done anything."

"Just let somebody enter and sit on a chair in front of you," I suggested. "You don't have to force it. They will appear."

"Do you have to write a letter or call someone on the phone to say you forgive them?" another man asked.

"If you need to write a letter, you should do it," I replied. "But you don't necessarily need to do it, because with the power of this prayer, you emanate forgiveness and compassion. You not only send it directly to the other person, but you send it out over the walls. This love and compassion emanates from you, from your beingness."

As the inmates started opening up to me, they shared with me how the guards treated them badly. It was always the guards' problem, not theirs. After teaching them the Forgiveness Prayer, the inmates mentioned that the guards had changed.

"Things are a lot different around there," they reported to me. "The guards are really great."

"It's not really the guards, is it?" I prompted. "Do you know who it is?"

"Yeah," they offered reluctantly. "It must be me."

The guards hadn't changed—it was the attitude of the inmates that had altered, without them even knowing it. The change was the change within them that comes from prayer.

The group started out with twenty-five inmates, but dwindled to eighteen and then nine by the end of the year. The ones who stayed were those who applied the process wholeheartedly. My favorite inmate was Sal. He was in prison for two years for robbing a bank. Every day, he'd wake up, do his twenty minutes of centering prayer, and then use the tape I'd given him to do the Forgiveness Prayer.

"Sal," I asked him during my monthly visit, "how are you doing?"

He looked excited, "Mary, you wouldn't believe what happened! I was going to take in my father because of our relationship that needs healing, but then this woman comes into my space. I haven't seen or heard from this woman in seventeen years. I told her to go away because my father was coming. She wouldn't go away. I had to do the Forgiveness Prayer with her."

"That's great, Sal," I responded. "She must be someone special in your life. What did you say to her?"

"I began to tell her how I thought she was responsible for this path I took, where I am today, for the problems in my life. When it came to forgiving her, I hesitated. I kind of spat it out, 'Okay, I forgive you.' Then I asked her how I'd hurt her and offended her, and she told me. Then I left for a closure to the prayer, and went back that evening again after I did my twenty minutes of centering prayer."

"Did she come back?"

"Yes! I had more to say to her. Then I forgave her again for what she did, and I asked her what I did, and she told me. I was so shocked at what she told me because it was true. I did all of those things."

I was happy at the progress Sal had made, but this wasn't the end of his story.

The following month, when I returned, he almost leaped up and down. "Mary, I got a letter from her! The woman I told you about, the one I hadn't seen in seventeen years. She wrote, 'Dear Sal, I have to write this letter to ask your forgiveness for what I've done in your life to you.' I got the letter here, Mary, you can read it during coffee break. Mary, what do you think happened?"

"Sal," I answered, "it was your forgiveness of her that invited her to reach out to you."

In helping all of these men come to terms with forgiveness, I had a realization similar to the one when I was holding my Bible Study groups. The reason I was in prison wasn't for the inmates to be healed—it was for *me* to be healed. Just as Sal had been contacted by the woman he'd forgiven, so I'd received that phone call from Joe after I'd truly forgiven him. Somehow, both parties had known that our barriers had been taken down, and that they were now free to reach out and seek their own reconciliation. I say, "Somehow," but I know it was the Holy Spirit at work.

Seeing what happened to Sal affirmed to me that I needed to be healed just as much as these prisoners. These men may have been criminals, but there'd been violence in my life too. That prison ministry was truly like a thousand hours of psychotherapy. Truly, I had been in a House of Correction.

But I wasn't finished in this particular house. Forgiveness had always been difficult for me, especially in regards to my husband and father. I'd forgiven Joe before his death in 1988; forgiving my father was much more difficult. But I perceived that the task had to be undertaken, if I was to be free from my own prison.

I did the Forgiveness Prayer over and over.

"Papa," I'd say. "Please come into my sacred space."

Eventually, my father stepped into the space, but I wasn't scared. I was aware that we were both in the presence of the spirit, and thus, in a safe place. I made known to him how the violent relationship between him and my mother had affected me.

"You didn't know you were hurting me when you were hurting my mother, did you?" I asked.

"I would never hurt you," my father said. "You were my precious, first-born little girl."

"But, Papa, you did."

I had to go through this process many times before I was finally able to say to my father the following words: *I forgive you. I forgive you. I forgive you.*

Shortly after I forgave my father, I read that for a child who is developing an identity, what happens to a person they love, happens to them. So the abuse that was inflicted on my mother was also inflicted on me. I also realized that the violence in my home when I was growing up had

179

contributed to the failure of my own marriage. I'd presumed the need to control my relationship with my husband so there wouldn't be any violence. All my life, I'd lived in fear of male violence because of my father.

Indeed, I'd never found unconditional love after my grandmother's death and in my marriage. I know my daughters felt I unconditionally loved them; they told me they felt that love when they were young. But I learned how to feel unconditionally loved with these inmates in my prison ministry. I think that as hardened as they were, and amidst all that potential violence, they reflected the same unconditional love back to me. Because of that, even when I had to pass through the high-security section of the prison, I was never afraid. It's part of the miracle of the Holy Spirit that the unsafe homes I'd lived in were finally reconciled with after I'd entered the most dangerous of environments and felt fully at home.

We're conditioned to think that we need to earn love, but love is *agape*—self-sacrificial, unconditional love, the highest kind in the Bible. In John 4:8 (the NIV Bible) says, "He who does not love does not know God; for God is love." Love is freely given by God, and that's what I received through the prison ministry.

I truly loved those men, and they loved me back.

10 Acceptance

For all that I was challenged and changed by my prison ministry, in many parts of my life, my old habits continued to assert themselves: after enlightenment, the dirty laundry, if you will. The need for security and acceptance, among other programs, manifested themselves in that most seditious and complex of impulses: my attitudes toward food.

My turkey dinners at Chrysalis House were legendary. As I wrote earlier, they were Fr. Keating's favorite, and I was sure to cook a bird whenever he visited. I basted the turkey overnight, and it was delicious. One time, David Frenette and Mary Dwyer were in charge of preparing the turkey. The only problem was that they'd never cooked one before. They were washing out the turkey according to the directions, and in the cavity were the gizzard and other innards. Not knowing what they were, David and Mary threw them out. When I tried to make the gravy, the pieces were nowhere to be found.

I let David and Mary have it. "What are we—rich, that we throw this out?" I scolded them.

Perhaps this should have been a sign that I had issues with food.

The act of cooking helped me process my emotions—banging pots and pans around while trying to work out problems. And the act of eating helped me even more. I loved food: preparing it, serving it, the full embodiment of it.

But I appreciated that my overeating was an addiction. It led to a poor self-image and poor self-esteem, as well as guilt, anger, and humiliation. These things, I realized, were all connected. On a physical side, the overeating contributed to my diabetes. The literal weight and the idea of it covered up my true self. When I began to eat inappropriately, I wasn't conscious or in the present moment. *Jesus, give me a healthy mind and body*, I prayed. I'd once been a smoker, and I judged my addiction to food to be very similar to my addiction to smoking. Once I stopped smoking cigarettes, I had no desire to take them up again. Food, however, was a different matter.

I kept food journals, in which I wrote, *"I give up my desire to control my weight"* and, *"Happiness and joy are better than insulin."* I kept a careful log of what I ate at every meal. My overeating was at its worst in 1989. I wanted to get my blood sugar down from 303 mg/dL to 93 mg/dL, and my weight from around 150 pounds to 110 pounds. My mother had died from diabetes, so I understood how dangerous it could be.

During this time, I developed wonderful friendships with two Cuban women who were interested in holistic healing. They were very concerned about my health, and in 1991, one of them offered to send me to the Hippocrates Health Institute in Florida, to get my diabetes and overeating under control. The Hippocrates Health Institute was just what I needed. It combined the mental process of changing eating habits with practical ways to do it. I was introduced to wheatgrass and whole foods, a raw diet and vegetable juices. I learned how to live without insulin.

I was on campus for three weeks, but it wasn't all strict living. During the final week, we took part in a cleanse. I lost weight and my skin glowed, as had happened to me when I'd participated in the Hindu cleanse with Connie Silveri years previously. You could see everyone else's skin glowing as well, because everyone was nude. A man there, who was blond and only thirty-five years old, even asked me if I wanted to have sex. That's how good I must have looked!

When I returned to Chrysalis House, I started on a wheatgrass kick. By default, everyone there adopted the same diet. We'd spend hours in the kitchen, cranking wheatgrass through an old metal juicer. I made salad dressings with nuts, and the only meat I ate was baked chicken. Mary Dwyer made poached chicken and once again, she was on the receiving end of my food wrath—I scolded her for trying to derail my diet. Mary understood my struggles, since she had her own issues with food. I did other things to improve my health, such as colonic cleanses and fasts. All of this, as well as the wheatgrass-and-raw diet, was expensive and I couldn't maintain it. But these methods worked. I lost weight, I no longer required the insulin, and I was in much better health. I was reinventing myself physically.

I'm aware that in putting my body through such extreme processes, I was in danger of falling into the same patterns of self-denial that the Buddha had rejected—the kind of self-denial that, as in the case of bulimics and anorectics, is a function of the need for control and power, in this case of one's body. On the other hand, I'd been abusing food by eating too much of it for a very long time. Furthermore, the medical profession had been abusing me by prescribing diet pills that effectively addicted me to amphetamines and caused me to lose weight and lose sleep. As with my practice of centering prayer, and my need to control every household I was in, I can't claim I fully conquered my demons when it came to food. But, at least, I became more aware of them!

With my body changing so much, perhaps it isn't a surprise that during this time, I had an out-of-body experience. That's the only way I can describe it. When visiting friends in Mexico, we decided to go camping and stayed in a primitive cabin in the mountains. The landscape was so pristine that we could drink water straight from the streams. We cooked over an open fire, and after dinner, we gazed at the stars and sank into a deep meditation. I'd never seen so many stars before. It was like they were spread across the sky like a twinkling blanket. As I admired their beauty, something in me shifted. In the midst of my meditation, I literally left my body. It was, as if attached by a sturdy string, I flew out of my physical being. I left the Earth and headed straight into the vast universe.

The moment I became fearful, I fell back into my body again. I looked around at my companions. They were all still in deep meditation and had no idea what had just happened to me. I didn't say anything about it to them. I didn't know if they'd believe me. I could hardly believe it myself. But when I returned to my regular life, I decided that it wasn't enough for my body to change. I needed to change my relationships too.

I deepened my connection to my sister, Fran, and my youngest brother, Peter. When I'd been living with Fran and her family, I relished being with them and their three daughters—Lorretta, Frances, and Angelina. Listening to them talk about their life was a very special time for me, and I can only hope I provided some sound counsel. Peter also asked me for advice about the oldest of his three sons, who was having trouble in high school.

"What did you do with the first teenager?" I asked him.

"What do you mean, the first teenager? This is my only teenager!" he replied.

"Well, you're raising a teenager," I continued. "You don't have any experience. This is your experience."

I reached out to my daughters and tried to be more patient and less judgmental with them and their families. Janet, her husband, and four children had been living in Maryland since 1988. In previous years, all my old patterns of control had emerged and I'd try to correct every little 'infraction' in the household to make it more like the one I remembered having. Every time I visited them, I would draw on my patience. *Dear God,* I prayed. *Give me your patience, your mercy.*

Once, when I visited them for Thanksgiving, Janet turned to me, "God, Mother, you're so patient."

"I am?" I asked. "What did I do? How was I patient?"

"It's wonderful the way you responded to Tony and the children. How did you do that?"

"What was I doing that was so patient?" I repeated, not understanding.

"You were just patient."

I guess I wasn't going to know what I did. I just replied, "Thank you, Janet. You know, it's been my prayer to be more patient."

"I'm not surprised. You were never that patient when I was a child."

This was true. *Now that's a real transformation*, I thought.

After that visit with Janet, I went to see Judith, who lived in Buffalo. The year Janet had moved to Maryland, Judith had married a psychiatrist. At first, she'd complained to me, "If I knew this was marriage, I wouldn't have gotten married. I had a perfectly good job and an apartment. What am I doing in this situation? My husband could be kinder and gentler. He's so self-centered..." She'd gone on and on in the same vein.

I hadn't wanted to tell Judith what to do. But finally, I retorted, "Judy, didn't you take the Open Mind Open Heart workshop with me twice?"

"Mother, are you telling me that I have a problem and not him?" she asked.

"Maybe."

After a while, Judith acknowledged, "Well, maybe you're right. I haven't really used that practice. But boy, does he tick me off!"

She returned to using the practice and later admitted it had helped her marriage.

On this visit at Thanksgiving, Judith blurted out, "Mother, you must have been given the gift of patience."

"Judy, have you been talking to your sister?" I exclaimed.

186

"No."

"Because that's exactly what she said to me."

I was amazed that, without discussing it beforehand, both my daughters had been able to see this fundamental change in me.

Judith's daughter, Bethany, was born in 1990. Because I was leading a retreat at the time, I wasn't able to be present for the birth. It was yet another major event in my daughters' lives that I'd missed. But even if my daughters sometimes seemed far away from me, and me from them, I let them know through my letters that they meant more to me than anyone on Earth.

> *I am so very happy that you have chosen me to be your mother. It's one issue for a woman to want to be a mother. It's even more important that the child chooses you to be a mother. I am a very fortunate and grateful woman.*
>
> *You mean more to me than life. Your presence in my life has given it meaning. What you have done in your life has given me joy. May you know that you are a very special creation that God has given to me and to the world. For whatever years are left for me, they shall be the icing on the cake. You are the entire cake for me. Just be who are… That is enough.*
>
> *I want you to know that I will be entering Holy Week with you and your family and hearts' desires in my prayers and in my heart. May this Easter be a new beginning for you. Enclosed is a piece of palm to remind you of freedom and interior level and space.*

The separation from you and my grandchild is so overwhelming. I sometimes feel like life has changed so drastically. It's like trying to reach you from another planet, and yet spiritually, I am there behind you. I pray for you all day long. You are in all my thoughts and feelings. I love you and admire you and your courage, faith, and trust.

That last letter was to Judith. Whenever I visited her house, I would retire upstairs after dinner because that was her time with her husband. Her husband would say to me, "I wish you would come more often because there's such a change when you're around." He offered to fix the upstairs of their house up for me to live in it. But, of course, I couldn't leave Chrysalis House. I didn't want to tell Judith how to live, but I supported her in her prayer practice. The relationship between her and her husband became calmer.

Throughout this time, I hadn't relinquished the idea of returning to a 'normal' life. I see it as no failure in my quest for an intimate relationship with God to admit that, sometimes, I wondered what it would be like if I left Chrysalis House after my last five-year commitment was up. Maybe I'd travel the world as a spiritual speaker. Or maybe I'd live in a nice house with geraniums on the porch, get remarried, and just live a happy life. I missed the physical intimacy and pleasure of a man's body—as well as the other gifts a man might be able to provide! As I wrote in my journal in 1992, *"I allow myself to marry a kind, generous, wealthy man in the New Year."*

That year was 1993.

That spring, Judith reconnected with her childhood friend, Antoinette Porretta. We hadn't heard from Antoinette for almost twenty years, since her mother, Helen, had passed away. Antoinette had left St. Mary-of-the-Woods College to take care of her younger siblings and father on Long Island.

I decided to visit Antoinette at her grandmother's house in Floral Park.

When she first saw me, she just stared. The last few times we'd been together, I'd been dressed in black, in mourning for my parents, my marriage, and her mother. Now I was vibrant in my red dress, red stockings, and high heels. It must have been like seeing someone you'd only known in black-and-white become Technicolor.

"Aunt Mary, you're with God!" she exclaimed.

For hours, Antoinette and I talked about her mother and the missed years, hardly stopping to eat or drink. It was important for me to let Antoinette, the daughter of my dear friend, know that she was unconditionally loved, just like my daughters.

Antoinette's sister, Cynthia, stopped by to say *hello*.

Unexpectedly, she asked, "Aunt Mary, are you afraid to die?"

"What is death?" I responded. "I'm not afraid. What are you going to be scared of? I don't know what's over there. I only know this place."

I didn't know that was the last time I would see Antoinette or Cynthia.

In May, I held a retreat with some nuns. We conducted an imaging prayer, and I saw myself as a little girl with Jesus holding me in his lap and rocking me like a baby. I remember the feeling I had at that age, being safe and warm with God. I distinctly heard him say, "Mary, it won't be long now."

In September, I accompanied Judith and her family on a trip to Greece for a scientific conference her husband was chairing. Afterward, they planned go to Italy. I'd visited Italy two years previously for my sixty-fifth birthday as a gift from Judith and Janet, and of course, I'd traveled with them, in 1975, to the International Congress for Charismatic Catholics in Rome.

In Greece, we first spent some time on the island of Rhodes where the conference was taking place. Judith's husband had helped organize one of the events, a celebration of the Jewish New Year in an old synagogue. The temple looked radiant and sacred in the midday sunshine, and I could feel the beauty and strength of this ancient tradition.

I was lost among the scientific crowd, so Judith, three-year-old Bethany, and I spent the rest of the time exploring the charming small towns and beaches of Rhodes. One day, we took a taxi to a beach at the end of the island. On the way, I chatted and laughed with the driver. When we reached our destination, I gave him a big tip.

"What are you doing?" Judith asked. "You just gave him twenty dollars."

"Sure did," I replied. "He's the only one who will talk to me during this trip!"

Then we flew to Palermo in Italy. We visited Mt. Etna, where I practiced Tai Chi on its famous slopes. This was like heaven to me. I was present in the moment, and it was exactly where I wanted to be—where there was no past and no future.

One evening, Judith's husband and a couple traveling with us decided to go look for a synagogue in Palermo, as they wanted to find a place for Rosh Hashanah services the next day. Judith, Bethany, and I arranged to meet up with them afterward and dined at a quaint little restaurant for dinner. Everything about that meal was special—the atmosphere, the attentive waiter, the delicious food, being with my daughter and little granddaughter. I couldn't stop gazing at Bethany and was very present with her.

After dinner, we strolled along the cobblestone streets and entered a cathedral. No one else was inside, and the smell of burning candles wafted to the arched ceiling.

Judith was looking at a painting of the Madonna. Suddenly, she turned to me and asked, "How could my biological mother give me up? I could have never given Bethany up at three days old."

I was taken aback. Judith had never asked about her biological mother before, and I'd never revealed to her anything except for the woman's last name and hair color, and some other family facts. For as long as I could remember, I'd been afraid of telling my daughters anything about their biological mothers, because I was terrified, I would lose them.

Now I said, "I loved your mother."

"What do you mean?" Judith asked.

"I loved her for giving you life and for giving you to me."

Judith turned back to the Madonna—the woman who'd given up her only son so that the entire world might be redeemed—and we continued to walk through the church with Bethany.

The next morning, the last day of our trip, I decided to rise early and buy some fruit for breakfast. As I walked down the cobblestone streets, I thought about my father, who'd come from a town in the south of Italy. Palermo was by the sea and Pietrelcina was in the mountains, but they probably looked similar.

Without warning, a speeding car passed me and knocked me against a stone wall and to the ground. A wave of pain, starting from my arm, pulsed throughout my body. As I lay crumpled on the ground, I immediately welcomed and let go of the desire to try to change what happened.

Welcome, pain. Welcome, pain. Welcome, pain.

The throbbing began to ease.

I let go of my desire to control the situation. I let go of my desire to control the situation. I let go of my desire to control the situation.

I sat on the ground and remained conscious throughout the ordeal. I was able to make myself understood with the police and directed them to the hotel. The hotel manager called Judith and for an ambulance. Judith accompanied me while her husband remained with Bethany. Judith yelled at the driver to slow down as he raced across, what seemed like every pothole in the street, afraid that the jostling would further injure my arm.

Throughout it all, I retained no expectations—whatever would happen would happen. All I could do was surrender. God provided me with clarity of mind and the ability to transmit what I somehow knew needed to be done. I didn't say, "God, change the pain. Heal my arm." That wasn't my work. My task was to focus, to welcome, and to surrender what happened, to God.

Thankfully, when I reached the hospital, I could understand some Italian, and we found someone who could help. My arm was broken. The doctor offered me painkillers but I waved them away. My letting-go practice was so strong that I didn't need them. The doctor looked at me in disbelief.

As my arm was being set, I couldn't help moving my feet back and forth.

"*Guardi, lei è ballare come una ballerina!*" a nurse exclaimed to the doctor. "Look, she's dancing like a ballerina!"

"*Io non solo una ballerina!*" I replied. "I'm not a ballerina!"

They were astonished that I understood what they were saying, and that I hadn't needed painkillers. I thanked them in Italian—*Grazie, grazie*—when the procedure was completed.

This wasn't the first time I'd used my letting-go practice to combat physical pain. I'd employed it when I hurt my lip that first year at Chrysalis House. A few years prior, I'd tripped on a step in the garden and broken my foot. I'd been due to speak in Los Angeles soon after, and had to postpone the trip. But I knew God would take care of all details—all I needed was to have trust and faith.

I trusted God in Palermo too, and as a result, I received a mystical experience, one of the greatest, most incredible of my life. I was surrounded by angels in the form of the people who helped me.

Just as when I'd broken my foot, when I broke my arm, I was scheduled to go on a speaking tour, this time to Denver, Colorado, and then Austin, Texas. My arm in a sling, I returned to Chrysalis House to rest for a few days before I left. I became very restless, as if something momentous was going to occur. Judith told me she was taking Bethany from New York City to Buffalo, and I begged her to stop by Chrysalis House on the way. At first, Judith confessed that she was too busy, but she eventually agreed to come.

That day was a Monday, our day off. David was out, and Cathy offered to do the chores so I could spend time with my family. I made Judith and Bethany soup, and we talked. I could sense that Judith was preoccupied and stressed about something. She admitted she was concerned that I was taking a trip with a broken arm and that the high altitude in Colorado might affect me.

I reassured her that the doctors had given me clearance to travel and that she should just let the matter go. I took Bethany down by the lake and gave her a little orange pumpkin in a light blue Tiffany's bag to take home. I was so glad I was able to spend some time with her.

Then I was off to Colorado. I stayed with Sr. Bernadette Teasdale, who'd helped establish Contemplative Outreach in that area. She lived in Georgetown, about an hour west of Denver. I loved visiting Sr. Bernadette. For the past eight years, I'd see her whenever I visited Snowmass, where Fr. Keating lived, and I taught her everything I'd learned about the Welcoming and Forgiveness prayers.

Sr. Bernadette and I also had fun on our own. We'd have dinner together and go dress shopping at Filene's Basement, where I acquired the best bargains. Sometimes, we'd go to the movies. Once, we went to see *Moonstruck*, starring Cher. The large New York Italian family in the movie was very familiar to me. Not only did I understand the Italian language, I recognized the characters' behavior so well, I could predict what someone would do before they did it. "Just watch, he's going to kiss her!" "Now she's going to slap him!" My asides kept Bernadette in stitches.

I traveled to Boulder, just thirty miles away, to give the Open Mind Open Heart workshop. During my talk, I related the story of what had happened to me in Palermo. The crowd was astonished at how I'd dealt with the pain.

"I never took an aspirin," I stated. "I welcomed and let go. But you have to remember: I've been doing this for a long time. It takes years of practice to be able to move through that kind of pain. You can do it with psychological pain, physical pain, and emotional pain. I'm going on eighteen, nineteen years of doing this practice, and I'm in awe of the life that it has. It's a real, viable prayer that's always developing. It's a live process and always changing."

The classroom I was lecturing in had a wide platform with a desk on top, and I was standing on the platform. At the break, a woman stepped forward to ask a question. She was quite insistent and moved closer. As I retreated, I fell off the platform, its edge hitting my head on my way down.

Blackness. I must have lost consciousness, because the next thing I was aware of, I was lying on the floor. People were surrounding me. I was in no pain and my mind was clear. So I advised them I didn't need to go to the hospital. I simply walked into the bathroom to wipe my face and returned. I spoke with people individually, and everything seemed fine.

On Sunday, Sr. Bernadette picked me up and drove me back to Georgetown. She'd heard what had happened and asked me if I wanted to see a doctor, but I insisted I was fine. I was scheduled on a flight out the next day anyway.

I was staying at the house of a parishioner who was often absent because she was a flight attendant. Sr. Bernadette was staying a block away in a one-bedroom house. On Monday morning, she picked me up and drove me back to her place. It was pleasant, with a stream that ran under the back porch, and a little chapel.

"How was your night?" Sr. Bernadette asked me.

"You know, I didn't sleep well," I admitted. "I was so restless. I'd tossed and turned for hours."

I knew centering prayer would help. We prayed in her chapel, ate breakfast, and then sat in her living room. Sr. Bernadette mentioned to me that she was having problems with a staff person and wanted advice. She really didn't know what to do about the situation, but I immediately recognized how to address it.

"I came here just for you," I told her.

I taught her a discerning method, where you look at the pros and cons of a situation, process it, and acquire a better perspective of what is actually happening. It's similar to the discernment process of St. Ignatius, where God's will becomes revealed. I do think this helped Bernadette.

We did this prayer practice, and prayer surrounded us, as it had throughout the morning when we were in the chapel, eating breakfast, and conversing together. At that moment, I'd never been so filled with prayer and so peaceful with my life, now that my spiritual journey was about to come to an end.

* * *

In the course of my life, I've learned that all we have is God and our spiritual practices. Centering prayer enabled me to hear and respond to God's invitation to have a personal and intimate relationship with Him. My consent, my *yes*, then opened me to be a receiver of unconditional love, because in my personal life, it was difficult for me to receive any kind of love.

In receiving this love through faith and trust, the fruits of centering prayer enabled me to love all of God's creatures unconditionally. I know now, with my entire being, that although we're all unique and different, we aren't separated from one another. We truly are all one in this ultimate mystery that we call God.

This surrender and giving myself to God—totally, completely, and intentionally—is essential to the spiritual journey. I've realized that returning to where I began is what the journey is about, on many levels and many dimensions. Returning to my origins is about being in and with God, as if I've gone back to the womb and every day I'm issued forth in this awareness and consciousness. Above all, I'm just a girl from Queens, New York, happy and free to share God's unconditional love with others.

I am very grateful for this journey.

Conclusion

The sun is shining—a cool breeze.
The meadows filled with color and light.
Today, I feel expansive, lite, and filled with life.
You ask who I am.
I am a hummingbird.
My rhythm is in the sound of movement.
I carry within me the sound of the universe.
It is not always known, but I am nurtured by the sweet life.
This is the movement of in and out and rest.
I have been very happy with my life.
The colors of my being are more vivid and pleasing to me.
These days, I live in harmony with myself and other creatures and the world around me. My being is in time and in touch with another dimension of life, as if the veil is parted and I fly in and out.

Being happy and free, I live to share life with others.
These days, with the music inside, as well as outside of my beingness.
In my tininess, I experience being a great capacity for love and life.

Because of my creatureliness, I know the truth that I am cared for and loved.
Unconditionally by my creator (GOD).

I was named many years ago…
The name given is,
SOPHIA.

My mother wrote this meditation shortly before she died. Sophia—the ancient Greek goddess of wisdom and the personification of the Hebrew, *Shekinah*—is the feminine dimension of God, and it might strike some as strange, even blasphemous, that Mary should associate herself with Sophia. How is it, some might ask, that she could call herself a hummingbird and talk about her 'tininess' and 'creatureliness' and yet, assign herself the role of wisdom incarnate?

Such a bifurcation of Mary's meditation misunderstands the nature of the revelation afforded to her in the final moments of her life. In reflecting on the sounds of the universe, in the movement of 'in' and 'out' (the inspiration and expiration of all creation), and in the heightened sensory awareness that marked her last days on this earth, we can detect the breath of God that fills all of his creatures. She is wholly of this world and yet, offered an awareness of 'another dimension of life' beyond the veil. She is, like the mustard seed mentioned by Jesus in Matthew 13:31-32, a minuscule vessel that contains the entire universe. She is present on this planet and at this time, and yet, she contains within her the essence of all of those who have been presented with a vision of their place amid the constant flow of God's revelation *within* the universe. In such a vision, Sophia's infinite receptivity to all that is creation, in her 'great capacity for love and life,' the nurturing, tolerant, and endlessly forgiving feminine aspect of God was expressed *through* my mother, as it can be through all of us, once we surrender to the creator of all things.

This was the Mary who, in the few days remaining to her, became present to us. She was transformed into a condition of pure transparency and joy. Every moment that she spent with us and with others, every gesture of her body, was an invocation to and of God's presence within and around us. People who saw Mary spoke of her interstitial state of existence, as if she was a vibrating membrane between the mundane and the eternal, this world and the next, the conditional and the absolute. It was as if she was connected to the divine to the fullest extent that we humans can tolerate without leaving our bodies permanently. The radiance that illuminated her was of a love that filled her up to overflowing; a love bestowed unreservedly and without end.

I understand that it's hard to comprehend just quite how she manifested that state of being. Those who've undergone near-death experiences or achieved illumination during meditation have likewise found it difficult to communicate just what it is they encountered. I'm also very aware, as a daughter, that Mary was reckless to assume that she had no need to see a doctor, following her fall off the stage—a legacy, as she admits in this book, of her wariness with the medical profession. On the other hand, having seen her in those last days and worried as any daughter would be about her mother's health, it's hard for me not to conclude that at some deep-psychic level, Mary was already leaving us for another plane.

Of course, such an observation is necessarily speculative, as much of this book has been, about what was transpiring in the deepest recesses of Mary's spiritual life. I'm aware that I wasn't privy to what she was experiencing, except to the extent that it showed itself in her body and in the lucid and compelling observations and counsel that she offered to those who came to see her at the end of her life. All I can offer in response to that skepticism is to say that, in my judgment—and in the judgment of many of those who came into contact with her—my mother was a saint.

Now, I can imagine that many of us might roll our eyes when someone is pronounced a saint. We might put the observation down to a loving daughter's rose-tinted views of her mother; or assume that 'my mother was a saint' is just another way of saying that Mary put up with a lot in her life, and did so without complaining; that she wasn't self-pitying, but was generous and oriented toward the welfare of other people. To a certain extent, that characterization has merit: she *did* undergo a lot of trials and tribulations; she *was* concerned about the welfare of others. But it's also true that my mother also wasn't afraid to lament what was happening to her, and there were times (especially when she brought my troubled brother into the family) where her concern for the welfare of others placed her other children at substantial risk. I hope that that very human, very fallible side of her, has come through clearly in this book.

In the popular imagination—fostered by innumerable images in stained-glass windows and hagiographies through the centuries—a saint is a man or woman, hands clasped in prayer, eyes lifted to the heavens, and with a halo circling their head. Or, as Thomas Keating said in his eulogy, the plaster saints in church. We may read about how they remained true to their faith in terrible circumstances, and how they were tortured or beaten or killed by authorities that refused to accept their beliefs, or that considered them so subversive that they were compelled to silence them. Likewise, when we think about what it means to be a 'sinner,' we may conjure up ideas of evildoers rubbing their hands in glee as they plan to perpetrate a crime, or people who visit unimaginable cruelties upon the innocent.

Yet, as my mother showed and Keating suggested, the holiness of a saint is not to be found in the explicitness of their piety or in a kind of neutered blandness. Mary was an earthy, brassy, even outrageous individual, who made lots of mistakes in her life—perhaps more than most. Far from being plain and sexless and contemptuous of this world and its so-called temptations, Mary was a fully embodied being, who liked material possessions and enjoyed and even flaunted her femininity. She had a warm and embracing presence, a robust sense of humor, and a strong temper.

She was also a sinner, in the way that *all* of us are sinners. We're all less-than-ideal individuals, prey to the pulls and pushes of our fallen human condition. There were times in her life that she lost contact with God, even moments as she herself acknowledged when she turned away from the heart of the faith that had sustained her. She was controlling and impulsive; stubborn and open to new possibilities; a woman who, all her life, searched for God and who struggled at every moment with resentment, fear, and an ego that craved acceptance and attention. But she kept on returning to God, and, eventually, was visited with the kind of hard-won and yet, paradoxically wholly unearned presence of the divine that we call *grace*, and which was so visibly expressed by her in her last years.

Her saintliness, therefore, had less to do with the travails that she was subject to in her life. It had more to do with the fact that, like the Samaritan woman at the well in John four, she wasn't afraid to approach Jesus and challenge him (and be challenged by him) on the meaning of faith. Like the Samaritan woman, she wasn't always appropriate. She didn't intone the scriptures in a measured manner, but had a thick New York accent and unvarnished guffaw. Like the Samaritan woman, she wasn't married for much of her life. Like the Samaritan woman, she ran afoul of the religious authorities, with their dictates about who is or who isn't an appropriate vessel for God's word.

Mary wasn't hidebound by liturgy or dogma, or the kind of Pharisaical nitpicking that stultifies belief and turns it into an account ledger of which rules and regulations you've followed and which you've bent or broken. Indeed, she didn't wait around to get the approval of the religious authorities. I recall how worried I was as a young woman in the 1970s, that Mary might be excommunicated for establishing the chapter of Divorced and Separated Catholics in the United States. But she shrugged off my concerns. People needed love and reassurance that God hadn't forgotten them because their marital relationship hadn't worked out. She certainly needed them, she reasoned, and if the Church wouldn't provide that love and reassurance, then she'd make sure she did.

That directness was another feature of my mother's sanctity. She was blunt and honest and open to everyone—even total strangers, such as prisoners, who were, in turn, touched by her acceptance and compassion. Her insights weren't pious platitudes, but practical and revealing (if sometimes uncomfortable for the person receiving them). She didn't preach or pronounce, but would instead step back and allow the person who'd come to her to hear and receive what she was saying, in their own way. In sum, she was entirely human—both sinner *and* saint—and thus, completely accepting of the divine expression of God's love.

If I have a blind spot about my mother, it comes from the fact that I grew up with her, filled with my own foolishness and false self—the one grasping for approval from others or seeking advantage over them; the one filled with vanity and self-regard. In other words, also human—like all of us. Like Mary. My sister and I have never forgotten that Mary shouldered a lot: the responsibility of being a father *and* a mother, taking in ironing to make ends meet (barely), living in and then leaving an abusive marriage, adopting and fostering children, and then losing her faith at the outset of her divorce. I'm forever grateful for her honesty. Even in the messiness of her life immediately before and after the divorce, she was never anything but real with us. Yes, she was opinionated and testy and direct. She believed in telling the truth without sugarcoating it. She perceived what needed to be said, but even when she chastised or corrected you, she did it with love—and, more importantly, you *knew* that she did it with love.

And that, I believe, is the final example of her saintliness: that, for the time that was allotted to her on this planet, she attempted to confront the world with candor. For her, truth was a form of prayer. Not supplication or penitence or propitiation, but an honest confrontation with our fallen human condition, a frank recognition of how vulnerable and weak we are, and then, an openness to the divine grace that is given so freely and so generously and which we have deserved so little. That surrender to the love of God, and that welcoming of his grace into her open mind and open heart, was never more present than in her final days. And together, they took her home.

Resources

Arico, Carl. *A Taste of Silence.* New York: Bloomsbury, 1999.

Bourgeault, Cynthia. *Centering Prayer and Inner Awakening.* Washington D.C.: Cowley Publications, 2004.

De Caussade, Jean-Pierre. *Abandonment to Divine Providence.* New York: Image Books, 1993.

Hall, Thelma. *Too Deep for Words.* Mahwah, New Jersey: Paulist Press, 1988.

Keating, Thomas. *The Better Part.* New York: Bloomsbury, 2007.

——. *Crisis of Faith, Crisis of Love.* New York: Continuum, 1995.

——. *Divine Therapy and Addiction: Centering Prayer and the Twelve Steps.* New York: Lantern Books, 2011.

——. *Fruits and Gifts of the Spirit.* New York: Lantern Books, 2000.

——. *The Heart of the World.* New York: Crossroad, 2008.

——. *The Human Condition.* Mahwah, New Jersey: Paulist Press, 1999.

——. *Intimacy with God.* New York: Crossroad, 2009.

——. *Invitation to Love: The Way of Christian Contemplation.* New York: Continuum, 2012.

——. *Manifesting God.* New York: Lantern Books, 2005.

——. *Meditations on the Parables of Jesus.* New York: Crossroad, 2010.

——. *The Mystery of Christ: The Liturgy as Spiritual Experience.* New York: Continuum, 1994.

——. *Open Mind, Open Heart: The Contemplative Dimension of the Gospel.* New York: Bloomsbury, 2006.

——. *Reflections on the Unknowable.* New York: Lantern Books, 2014.

——. *St. Therese of Lisieux: A Transformation in Christ.* New York: Lantern Books, 2001.

Keating, Thomas, Cynthia Bourgeault, and Beatrice Bruteau. *Spirituality, Contemplation, and Transformation: Writings on Centering Prayer.* New York: Lantern Books, 2008.

Keating, Thomas, *et al. The Divine Indwelling: Centering Prayer and Its Development.* New York: Lantern Books, 2001.

Lawson, Paul David. *Old Wine in New Skins: Centering Prayer and Systems Theory.* New York: Lantern Books, 2001.

Maslow, Abraham. *Motivation and Personality.* New York: Harper & Row, 1954.

May, Gerald G. *Addiction and Grace.* San Francisco: HarperOne, 2007.

Ó Madagáin, Murchadh. *Centering Prayer and the Healing of the Unconscious.* New York: Lantern Books, 2011.

Peele, Norman Vincent. *The Power of Positive Thinking*. New York: Touchstone, 2003.

Pennington, Basil. *Centering Prayer*. New York: Image Books, 1982.

Tasto, Maria. *The Transforming Power of Lectio Divina*. New London, Connecticut: Twenty-Third Publications, 2013.

The Welcoming Prayer

By Mary Mrozowski

Gently become aware of your body and your interior state.

Welcome, welcome, welcome.

I welcome everything that comes to me in this moment because I know it is for my healing.

I welcome all thoughts, feelings, emotions, persons, situations, and conditions.

I let go of my desire for security.

I let go of my desire for approval.

I let go of my desire for control.

I let go of my desire to change any situation, condition, person, or myself.

I open to the love and presence of God and His healing action and grace within.

The Forgiveness Prayer

By Mary Mrozowski

Begin with a period of centering prayer.

Following this, spend a few moments in silence.

Close your eyes and gently ground yourself in your body; scan your body with your inner eye and relax each part of your body.

Rest in the area of your chest near your heart. Breathe.

Focus on your heart and allow your heart to open. Breathe the light of the Spirit into your heart. Open.

Continue to relax into your body…

Gently allow the Spirit to lead you through a passageway that is filled with light, warmth, and a welcoming presence.

Invite the Holy Spirit to bring forth a person, living or dead, whom you need to forgive.

Remain open to whomever appears in your sacred place. Greet the person by name.

Share your experience of being in a relationship with this person; share how you have been hurt, offended, traumatized. Be specific.

Allow yourself to share your pain with this person. Relax in the process and remain open.

Relax in the process and remain open.

When you feel ready, tell the person that you forgive them. Gently say, "I forgive you. I forgive you. I forgive you." Repeat as many times as needed, until you feel ready to continue the process.

Now ask the person how you have offended, traumatized, or hurt them.

Wait and listen.

Remain open to the process.

When you feel ready, gently say, "Forgive me. Forgive me. Forgive me." Repeat as many times as needed, until you feel complete in the process for now. Observe your thoughts, feelings, and emotions. Just be present with them.

Allow the person to leave your sacred, safe place. Invite the person to return at a later time if needed.

Rest in the spirit. Take as much time in silence as you wish.

Prepare the leave your sacred place. Move out of the sacred place...through the door into the passageway...grounded in your body. Gently open your eyes when you feel ready.

Close with a prayer.